Equal Pay in the Office

Equal Pay in the Office

Francine D. Blau
University of Illinois

Lexington Books
D.C. Heath and Company
Lexington, Massachusetts
Toronto

331.4
B64e

Am

Library of Congress Cataloging in Publication Data

Blau, Francine D.
  Equal pay in the office.

  Includes bibliographical references.
  1. Equal pay for equal work—United States. 2. Women—Employment—
United States. 3. Sex discrimination against women—United States.
4. Labor supply—United States. I. Title.
HD6061.B5   331.4'2'0973   76-55077
ISBN 0-669-01003-0

Published simultaneously in Canada.

Printed in the United States of America.

International Standard Book Number: 0-669-01003-0

Library of Congress Catalog Card Number: 76-55077

For my parents

Contents

List of Tables

Acknowledgments

In the preparation of this book, I have benefited greatly from the advice and assistance of a variety of individuals and agencies. Peter Doeringer and Richard Freeman, at Harvard University, contributed many excellent suggestions and insights. I am also grateful to Lawrence Kahn for his advice and moral support in the revision of the manuscript for publication. Others to whom I am indebted for their helpful comments and valuable suggestions include Heidi Hartmann, Carol Jusenius, Richard Nelson, Andrew Kohen, Barbara Bergmann, Gilbert Nestel, Vahid Nowshirvani, Christopher Heady, Louis Silversin, Ann Freedman, Marianne Ferber, and Wallace Hendricks. I would like to acknowledge a special debt to the late Peggy Howard for her role in stimulating my initial interest in the subject of this book and in shaping my approach to the problems investigated here.

The Bureau of Labor Statistics made this study possible by generously granting me access to the unpublished data collected for the *Area Wage Surveys*. I would especially like to thank Samuel Cohen and John Gracza for their role in making the data tape available and assisting me in its use.

I am indebted to Christopher Heady and Donna Lustgarten for ably undertaking the major part of the computer work necessary for the completion of this project. Thanks are due to Sylvia Moore and Kathryn Ross for their valuable research assistance. I would like to express my gratitude to the Center for Human Resource Research of the Ohio State University and to the Institute of Labor and Industrial Relations and the Department of Economics of the University of Illinois at Urbana-Champaign for facilitating the completion of this study.

Portions of the material in this project were prepared under Grant No. 91-25-71-24 from the Manpower Administration, U.S. Department of Labor, under the authority of Title I of the Manpower Development and Training Act of 1962, as amended. Since researchers undertaking such projects are encouraged to express their own judgment freely, this study does not necessarily represent the official opinion or policy of the Department of Labor.

Equal Pay in the Office

1 Introduction

The issue of pay differentials between male and female workers has recently become the focus of considerable theoretical interest and empirical research. For the most part, empirical studies in this area have attempted to estimate the extent of wage discrimination by sex in the labor market. Wage discrimination against women may be said to exist when the ratio of male to female wages is greater than the ratio that would result in the absence of discrimination (Becker, 1957, p. 9).

In empirical work, the general practice has been to estimate the proportion of the male-female pay differential that is attributable to differences in those characteristics of male and female workers that are related to productivity. The residual, or unexplained portion of the differential, is then ascribed to discrimination.[1] A recent review of seven studies of male-female pay differences found that in six cases the unexplained earnings gap was estimated at between 29 percent and 43 percent of male earnings (Sawhill 1973, pp. 387, 391). The exception, a study by Sanborn, found a differential of 12 percent after standardizing for detailed occupational classification (1964, p. 535).[2]

The existence of large pay differentials between male and female workers that cannot be attributed to individual differences in productivity-related characteristics, and the large reduction in the size of the unexplained differential when detailed occupational classifications are taken into account have led a number of scholars to focus on the prevalence of sex segregation in the labor market.[3] The existence of sex segregation has generally been deduced from aggregate census data which indicate that a large number of detailed occupational categories tend to be either predominantly male or predominantly female, and that such segregated occupations involve relatively high proportions of the male and female labor forces respectively. For example, in 1970, 73 percent of female workers (as contrasted with 10 percent of male workers) were in detailed census classifications in which women constituted 50 percent or more of the incumbents; on the other hand, 80 percent of male workers (as contrasted with 16 percent of female workers) were in occupations whose composition was less than 30 percent female.[4] A pay differential between men and women with similar productivity-related characteristics is commonly seen to result from this labor-market segmentation, and the consequent "overcrowding" of the female sector.

The purpose of this book is to shed further light on the causes and consequences of sex segregation in the labor market by going to the level of establishment to examine the relationship of differences in the employment

1

distribution of male and female workers among firms to the male-female pay differential within selected white-collar occupations. In contrast to earlier studies, the establishment rather than the individual is taken as the unit of analysis. This approach makes it possible to examine data at the level of disaggregation at which many of the employment decisions which produce the observed patterns of employment segregation and pay differences are made. The use of establishment data permits us to observe the employment and pay practices of the firm across a variety of occupations, thus providing a fertile field within which to test a number of hypotheses concerning employer behavior.

This study also differs from earlier empirical work in the types of wage questions that are considered. The purpose is not to estimate what proportion of specific differentials between men and women workers may be attributed to discrimination. Rather, an effort is made to delineate the broad pattern of the relationship of differences in the distribution of men and women workers among establishments to male-female pay differentials, and to suggest reasonable hypotheses concerning the behavior which produces this pattern.

Analyses of employer discrimination generally proceed from an assumption of perfect competition in the labor market. However, in our view, the role of employer preferences can best be understood within a model that takes explicit account of the institutional and market constraints under which employers operate. Two types of constraints are considered to be of particular importance.

First are institutional considerations internal to the firm that place limits on the employer's ability to differentiate among individuals, and thus between men and women. Specifically, the employer is seen as being constrained to pay the same base pay rate to all workers within an occupational category. Wage differentiation among individuals within occupational categories is limited to seniority and merit considerations. In addition, the employer is believed to face a relatively rigid internal wage structure which specifies wage relationships among occupational categories.

Second are institutional and market considerations that determine the position of the establishment in the labor-market wage hierarchy. Given the interrelationships among occupational wage rates and the necessity of equal base occupational pay rates for both sexes, the relative wage position of the firm is postulated as being consistent across occupational categories and sex groups.

These factors are seen as operating on the demand side to yield a structure of occupational wage rates that may be offered by the firm, regardless of the sex of the worker employed. The wage relationships specified by the internal wage structure and the position of the firm in the wage hierarchy of establishments are shaped by a variety of factors and cannot easily be altered to accommodate employer preferences regarding the sex composition of specific occupational categories. Thus it is argued that while the preference for male over female labor is fairly widespread, the employer's ability to exercise this preference is constrained by the position of the establishment in the interfirm wage hierarchy.

In each occupational category, male workers are primarily sought by and attracted to the higher-wage establishments, while female workers are likely to find employment in the lower-paying firms which, regardless of their preferences, are less able to compete for male labor.

The empirical investigation proceeds at two levels. First, at the level of the occupational category, the extent to which male and female workers are segregated by firm is ascertained, and the relationship of sex differences in employment distributions to the intraoccupational pay differential is examined. Second, at the level of the establishment, we examine the extent to which firms exhibit consistent patterns with respect to the representation of women in the establishment work force and the pay rates of employees, both across occupational categories, and the relationship of such interfirm differences in employment patterns and pay rates to a variety of economically meaningful establishment characteristics.

Given the high proportion of pay differences explained by occupational segregation, such differences between male and female workers in the same detailed occupational categories can account for only a small fraction of the aggregate pay differential between men and women in the labor market. Nonetheless, an understanding of the impact of distributional factors on male-female pay differences within occupational categories has considerable importance.

Different occupational categories may be thought of as requiring or emphasizing different training, skills, and abilities, although certainly some overlap exists in specific cases. Thus an explanation of the differences in the distribution of men and women among occupations would necessarily be exceedingly complex and would require some assessment of the impact of a large number of factors including early socialization and possibly even innate sex-linked characteristics, the role of educational institutions, historical forces, differing preferences of workers by sex group, and the existence of various types of discrimination. Differences in the distribution of men and women among firms *within* occupational categories, since they occur among individuals of similar training, skills, and abilities, provide an opportunity to test some simpler hypotheses concerning the causes of segregation, which may then shed some light on the causes of segregation by occupation as well.

The interpretation of wage differences may be less ambiguous within occupational categories where workers are relatively homogeneous. Examining pay data at the establishment level permits us to discern the pattern of the wage consequences of employment segregation within such homogeneous groups of workers.

An understanding of the scope and implications of sex segregation in employment requires some knowledge of its depth and dimensions. At present, little evidence exists regarding the extent of sex segregation by establishment within occupational categories. Further, it is not known whether establishments

exhibit consistent patterns in the degree of utilization of women across
occupational categories, or what characteristics of establishments are important
in determining the sex composition of employment. This study is designed to
extend our knowledge in these areas.

Information presently available is inadequate for the formulation of policies
to reduce the income disparity between men and women in the labor market.
While we may advocate the integration of presently segregated occupations, we
know little about the problems that will remain after such integration is
accomplished. Since this study is concerned with differences in the employment
distribution and pay rates of men and women within occupational categories, it
may be helpful in this respect.

Scope of Study and Source of Data

The focus of this study is upon pay differentials and differences in the
distribution of employment of male and female office workers in three large
northeastern standard metropolitan statistical areas: Boston, New York, and
Philadelphia. A wide variety of clerical, professional, and technical occupations
are included in the sample. Occupations are narrowly defined and generally
subdivided into skill classifications. A complete list of the occupations and job
definitions is presented in Appendix A.

The data used in this study were collected by the Bureau of Labor Statistics
for the *Area Wage Surveys* between April and November of 1970. The data
provide information about standard weekly earnings and hours by sex and job
category as well as by certain characteristics of the establishment including type
of industry, size of firm, and union status of a majority of plant and office
workers. Since B.L.S. field investigators classify workers by occupational
category and skill grade, comparability across establishments is maximized.
Working supervisors, apprentices, learners, beginners, trainees, and handicapped,
part-time, temporary, and probationary workers are excluded from the sample by
field investigators. The occupational-skill-class pay rates employed in this study
are computed as standard weekly earnings divided by standard weekly hours and
will be referred to as the *wage*. Overtime payments are not included in the
estimate of earnings.

Types of Employment Segregation by Sex

Since we are concerned with the relationship of differences in the employment
distribution of men and women to pay differentials by sex, it is helpful to
clearly distinguish the dimensions of sex-segregation in employment, and to
identify the types of segregation that are of particular relevance to the wage

questions addressed in this study. In this section we define four types of employment segregation and illustrate the relationships among them.

Interoccupational segregation. Male and female workers may be differentially distributed among occupational categories. The criterion for the existence of interoccupational segregation is the extent of the divergence between the representation of women in specific occupational categories and their representation in the total labor force. The greater the divergence, the more segregated the occupation is considered.

Intraoccupational segregation. Within occupational categories, male and female workers may be differentially distributed among establishments. Intraoccupational segregation is determined by the divergence between the representation of women in the occupational work force of the individual establishment and their representation in the total occupational work force. The criterion for the existence of intraoccupational segregation is whether in given occupational categories women tend to work with women (and men with men) within the same establishment to a significantly greater extent than would occur according to chance.

Establishment segregation. Male and female workers may be differentially distributed among establishments when occupational categories are considered jointly. The criterion for the existence of establishment segregation is whether members of a sex group in different occupations work together within individual establishments to a significantly greater extent than would result from a random distribution of all members of each occupation among establishments. Stated somewhat differently, establishment segregation requires consistent patterns of high or low representation of women across occupational categories in a firm.

Industry segregation. Male and female workers may be differentially distributed among industries when establishment employment patterns are considered jointly. The criterion for the existence of industry segregation is whether establishments that exhibit similar employment patterns with respect to the representation of women across occupational categories are located within specific industry groups to a greater extent than would result from a random distribution of all establishments among industries. That is, industry segregation requires consistent patterns of high or low representation of women across establishments within industry groups. Establishment and industry segregation as we have defined them may be considered as two dimensions of what Becker (1957, p. 49) has termed "market segregation." He states, "In general, if various members of different factors (such as laborers and foremen) are combined into one group by a criterion such as color or religion, one can say that market segregation of this group exists if its members are employed with each other to a significantly greater extent than would result from a random distribution of all members of each factor."

The four types of segregation that we have identified are all symmetrical in the sense that the segregation of one sex group implies the segregation of the other. However, the economic consequences of segregation need not be the same for both groups and, indeed, we do not expect them to be. The definitions of intraoccupational, establishment, and industry segregation take as given the magnitude of interoccupational segregation, that is, the proportion that women comprise of total employment in each occupational category. Thus, there is no necessary relationship between the existence or extent of interoccupational segregation and the existence or extent of any of the three other types of segregation. The latter group, however, do bear a necessary relationship to each other. The existence of intraoccupational segregation is a necessary but not a sufficient condition for the existence of establishment segregation, while establishment segregation is a necessary but not a sufficient condition for the existence of industry segregation.

An Illustrative Example: Interoccupational
and Intraoccupational Segregation

The relationship between interoccupational and intraoccupational segregation can be most easily illustrated by a simple set of examples for a hypothetical two-firm, two-occupation situation, as shown in Table 1-1. N_{mi} and N_{fi} represent the number of men and women respectively in the occupational category in the ith firm, while P_{fi} is the proportion that women comprise of the establishment's occupational work force. The figures under the "Market-Wide" heading are the total numbers of each sex employed in the occupation and the proportion which women constitute of all incumbents of the category. Assuming that women comprise 40 percent of the total labor force, four cases are distinguished.

In Case 1, there is no segregation of either type. Women comprise 40 percent of the labor force of each occupational category in the aggregate and in both establishments. In Case 2, there is interoccupational segregation, but no intraoccupational segregation. Occupation A and Occupation B are disproportionately female and disproportionately male respectively. However, the representation of women in each of the occupations within both firms is identical to their representation at the aggregate level. In Case 3, there is intraoccupational segregation, but no interoccupational segregation. At the aggregate level, the representation of women in each occupation is identical to their proportion of the total labor force. However, within the establishment each occupation is either disproportionately male or disproportionately female relative to the representation of each sex in the total occupational employment. Occupation A

Table 1-1

An Illustration of the Relationship Between Interoccupational and Intraoccupational Segregation

	Firm 1			Firm 2			Market-wide		
	N_{m1}	N_{f1}	P_{f1}	N_{m2}	N_{f2}	P_{f2}	N_m	N_f	P_f
Case 1: No Segregation									
Occupation A	60	40	0.40	30	20	0.40	90	60	0.40
Occupation B	6	4	0.40	15	10	0.40	21	14	0.40
Case 2: Inter-No Intra									
Occupation A	10	90	0.90	5	45	0.90	15	135	0.90
Occupation B	45	5	0.10	90	10	0.10	135	15	0.10
Case 3: Intra-No Inter									
Occupation A	0	40	1.00	60	0	0.0	60	40	0.40
Occupation B	55	5	0.08	5	35	0.88	60	40	0.40
Case 4: Inter and Intra									
Occupation A	0	80	1.00	20	0	0.0	20	80	0.80
Occupation B	5	15	0.75	75	5	0.07	80	20	0.20

illustrates complete intraoccupational segregation and Occupation B a significant level of this type of segregation. Case 4 exhibits the presence of both forms of segregation. Women are either over- or underrepresented in each occupation relative to their share of total employment and over- to underrepresented in the establishment's occupational labor force relative to their share of total occupational employment.

Table 1-1 is also useful in illustrating the relationship between intraoccupational segregation and establishment segregation. It is apparent that establishment segregation can only occur in Cases 3 and 4, where intraoccupational segregation is present. Establishment segregation can be said to exist if the proportion that women represent in establishment employment in Occupation A is positively correlated with their representation in Occupation B. This example, in which establishment segregation is present in Case 4 but not in Case 3, illustrates the point made earlier that the existence of intraoccupational segregation is a necessary but not a sufficient condition for the existence of establishment segregation. Table 1-1 also indicates the limitations of using aggregate census data to measure labor market segregation. Such limitations would not affect the results in Cases 1 and 2, where there is no intraoccupational segregation. However, in Cases 3 and 4, census data would underestimate the true extent of labor market segregation.

*An Illustrative Example: Establishment
and Industry Segregation*

The relationship between establishment and industry segregation may be illustrated by a simple set of examples for a hypothetical two-occupation, four-firm, two-industry situation, as shown in the first three cases of Table 1-2. In these cases, intraoccupational segregation—which we know to be a necessary condition for the other types of segregation—is present. Interoccupational segregation is also present in these cases: Occupation A is predominantly female and Occupation B predominantly male. We have used relatively segregated occupations in this illustration simply to emphasize the point that the representation of women within an establishment's occupational work force must always be judged relative to the proportion that women comprise of total occupational employment. (For example, the occupations of typist and secretary are almost all female, whereas the occupations of engineer and draftsman are predominantly male.)

In Case 1, neither establishment nor industry segregation is present. In each establishment, women are either over- or underrepresented in the occupational work force of the firm relative to their share of total occupational employment, but the pattern is not consistent across occupational categories. Since no consistent establishment patterns emerge, consistent industry patterns are not

Table 1-2

An Illustration of the Relationship Between Establishment Segregation and Industry Segregation

	Industry X		Industry Y	
	P_{f1}	P_{f2}	P_{f3}	P_{f4}
Case 1: No Segregation of Either Type				
Occupation A ($P_f = .60$)	0.80	0.30	0.90	0.20
Occupation B ($P_f = .20$)	0.10	0.60	0.05	0.70
Case 2: Establishment-No Industry				
Occupation A ($P_f = .60$)	0.80	0.30	0.90	0.20
Occupation B ($P_f = .20$)	0.50	0.10	0.60	0.05
Case 3: Establishment and Industry				
Occupation A ($P_f = .60$)	0.80	0.90	0.30	0.20
Occupation B ($P_f = .20$)	0.50	0.60	0.10	0.05
Case 4: No Segregation of Either Type				
Occupation A ($P_f = .60$)	0.60	0.60	–	–
Occupation B ($P_f = .20$)	–	–	0.20	0.20
Occupation C ($P_f = .40$)	0.40	0.40	0.40	0.40

possible. Thus we see that establishment segregation is a necessary condition for the existence of industry segregation. Case 2 illustrates a situation in which there exists establishment, but not industry, segregation. In each of the four establishments, employment patterns are consistent across occupations. Women are either over- or underrepresented in both Occupation A and Occupation B: establishment segregation is thus present. However, establishment employment patterns are not consistent within industry groups. For example, in the case of Industry X, women are disproportionately overrepresented in both occupations in Firm 1, while in Firm 2 women are underrepresented in both occupations. Thus we see that establishment segregation is not a sufficient condition for industry segregation. Case 3 exhibits both establishment and industry segregation: in Industry X, women are overrepresented in both occupations, in both firms; in Industry Y, women are underrepresented in both occupations, in both firms.

Case 4 has been added to emphasize the fact that the average proportion that women comprise of establishment employment is not a correct measure of establishment segregation, nor is the average female share of industry employment a correct measure of industry segregation. Women may comprise a high or low proportion of total establishment or industry employment simply because of the occupational mix of the establishment or industry. In Case 4, the firms in

Industry X employ no workers in Occupation B, a predominantly male job, while the firms in Industry Y employ no workers in Occupation A, a predominantly female job. Women will certainly comprise a higher proportion of total employment in Industry X firms than in Industry Y firms, yet there exists no intraoccupational, establishment, or industry segregation.

Summary

This study is devoted to the analysis of intraoccupational segregation, as illustrated in Cases 3 and 4 of Table 1-1, and establishment and industry segregation, as illustrated in Cases 2 and 3 of Table 1-2. These types of segregation take the magnitude of sex segregation by occupations, the primary focus of earlier work, as given.[5] Thus, intraoccupational, establishment, and industry segregation may theoretically exist in the presence or absence of interoccupational segregation. However, the extent of interoccupational segregation in the labor market is, in fact, an open empirical question.

Trends in the Magnitude of Segregation by Occupation, 1950-1970

Although we are primarily concerned in this study with an analysis of intraoccupational, establishment, and industry segregation, it is important to describe, in summary, the extent of interoccupational segregation in order to illuminate the broader market context within which the other types of segregation exist. Therefore, we review the trend between the years 1950 and 1970 in the degree of sex segregation by occupation, and offer explanations for the observed changes in its magnitude during this period. This review of the trends in the extent of interoccupational segregation utilizes decenial census data which were collected at different points in the business cycle. In the absence of detailed occupational information for intervening years, we are not able to examine the possibility of cyclical sensitivity in the degree of segregation.

The Measurement of Segregation by Occupation

When considering the changes in degree of interoccupational segregation over time, it is often helpful to employ some summary measure for degree of segregation. One such indicator is the Index of Segregation devised by Duncan and Duncan (1955, pp. 493-503).[6] It has been used in the measurement of both occupational and residential segregation. The Index of Segregation may be calculated from the detailed census occupational distributions of males and females in the experienced labor force. (It is computed as the sum of the absolute differences between the proportion of the male labor force and the proportion of the female labor force in each census category, divided by two.) It may take on any value between zero and 100. A value of zero indicates that the distribution of women across occupations is identical to that of men or, similarly, that the proportion which women comprise of those employed in each occupational category is the same as women's share of the total labor force. A value of 100 indicates complete segregation, with women employed in exclusively female categories and men working in entirely male occupations. The actual value of the Index may be interpreted to be the percentage of women (or men) who would have to change occupations in order for the employment distribution of the two groups to be identical.

The computed value of the Index was 65.6 in 1950, 68.4 in 1960, and 65.8 in 1970.[7] Thus, in each census year, roughly two-thirds of the female labor force would have had to be reallocated to eliminate the overrepresentation of women in certain occupations and their underrepresentation in others. (Gross (1968, p. 202) found a similar stability in the value of the Index over the whole period from 1900 to 1960.) While the value of the Index has fluctuated slightly from census year to census year, simultaneous changes in the census classification scheme make such small changes difficult to evaluate. In general, the effect of the classification changes has been to create more detailed occupational categories and thus to facilitate the detection of sex segregation by occupation. For example, in the 1950 census, barbers, beauticians, and manicurists formed one job category, which was 50 percent female in composition. When the data were reclassified, however, so that hairdressers and cosmetologists formed a separate category, 92 percent of this group were women (Oppenheimer 1970, p. 67).

Changes in the Extent of Segregation by Occupation

To determine with some precision the trends in the magnitude of sex segregation by occupations, it is necessary to remove the biases introduced by changes in census classifications. We have computed the employment distributions of male and female workers across 183 occupational categories for which it was possible to obtain comparable data in each census year. With the exception of a general nonfarm laborer group, each of these occupations comprises a detailed census classification or a combination of closely related classifications (for example, the various classifications of medical doctors were grouped into one "physicians and surgeons" category). In the interests of accuracy, and clarity of interpretation, we have not formed categories such as "other clerical workers" or "other operatives" in an attempt to account for the entire male and female labor force. However, the included occupations represent a large and relatively stable proportion of men and women in the experienced civilian labor force (Table 1-3). While our estimate of the magnitude of segregation may differ from an estimate based on the full set of census classifications, measured trends over time in the degree of segregation based on our sample of occupations should be representative of changes in the actual magnitude of segregation in the labor force as a whole.

The results of this analysis are presented in Table 1-3. While a substantial amount of segregation by occupation was present in all three census years, there were some small changes in the magnitude of segregation over the two decades. The use of comparable occupational categories permits us to report these changes with some degree of confidence. Between 1950 and 1960, the Index of Segregation increased by 2.2 percentage points, whereas between 1960 and 1970, the Index declined by 3.4 percentage points to slightly below the 1950 level. The Council of Economic Advisors found a decrease of 3.1 percentage points in the Index of Segregation between 1960 and 1970. This estimate was based on a comparable group of occupations in the two years. Although, in contrast to our procedure, the Council's study included broad residual occupational categories, the two approaches appear to produce similar measures of changes in the level of segregation (Economic Report of the President 1973, p. 155).

The decline in the measured degree of segregation in 1970 was due to a greater diffusion of male workers throughout the occupational distribution rather than to a reduction in the concentration of women in predominantly female jobs.

In both 1950 and 1960, approximately 83 percent of male workers reported belonging to occupations of which 20 percent or less of the incumbents were female. By 1970, this figure had declined to 74 percent. Similarly, the proportion of men in occupations which were 21-40 percent female rose from 6 percent in 1950 to 12 percent in 1970.

This shift in the distribution of male workers helped to offset the impact of the increasing concentration of women workers in occupations that were 81-100 percent female. The proportion of women in occupations in this sex composition group was 54 percent in 1950, 58 percent in 1960, and 61 percent in 1970. While a small secular increase occurred in the proportion of men in these predominantly female occupations (notably in the 81-90 percent group), it was not sufficient to counterbalance the increasing disparity in the representation of men and women in the two extreme groupings combined (81-90 percent and 91-100 percent).

While Table 1-3 provides a useful summary of the degree of segregation in each census year, the factors responsible for the observed changes are not readily discernible. The difficulty is that changes in the proportion that women comprise of an occupational category arise for a variety of reasons. However, any change of considerable magnitude in the sex ratio in an occupational classification, regardless of its source, will cause a reclassification of the incumbents of the occupation in terms of sex composition category.

Throughout the period under study, women's share of the experienced work force was rising, due to secular increases in the female labor force participation rate. Thus the proportion which women comprise of occupational categories that maintain a constant relative share of the male and female labor force would also be expected to rise. Even in cases where changes in the sex composition of occupational categories are due to changes in the occupational distribution of men or women, it is not immediately obvious from Table 1-3 which sex group has undergone occupational change. For example, between 1950 and 1960 there was a decline of 6 percentage points in the proportion of women in occupations which were 91-100 percent female. This change was primarily due to an increase in the participation of men in the elementary school teaching profession. Women comprised 91 percent of elementary school teachers in 1950, as compared to 86 percent in 1960 (they comprised 84 percent of elementary school teachers in 1970). This occupation contained roughly the same proportion of all women workers in both years.

The Impact of Changes in the Occupational Distribution of Male and Female Workers

We are interested in identifying the major occupational changes in male and female employment that have produced the observed trends in the degree of segregation. Because of the problems mentioned earlier, it is helpful to employ a constant frame of reference to net out the impact of increases in the female share of the labor force, and to uncover the important occupational changes. Table 1-4 shows the distribution of men and women according to the sex composition of the occupational category in 1950. While there have been numerous changes in the sex composition of specific occupational classifications over the twenty-year period, we shall focus on those shifts with the largest impact.

The data in Table 1-4 indicate that it was not until after 1960 that a decline occurred in the concentration of men in occupations which were between 0 and 10 percent female in 1950. Between 1960 and 1970, the proportion of men in this group of occupations fell from 72 percent to 68 percent. This decrease was primarily due to certain long-term shifts in the structure of the economy having a major impact on occupations in this sex composition category.

There has been a decline, for example, in the relative importance of agricultural employment. The proportion of men in the sample who were farmers, farm managers, farm foremen, or farm wage laborers was 21 percent in 1950 as compared to 7 percent in 1970. There has also been a decrease in the proportion of workers who are unskilled nonfarm laborers. This job category

Table 1-3

Distribution of Men and Women by Sex Composition of Occupational Category in Each Year: 1950, 1960, 1970[a]–Experienced Civilian Labor Force, age 14 and over

(Percentages)

Sex composition category (Women as a percentage of total in occupation)	1950			1960			1970		
	Men	Women	Women as a percentage of total in sex composition category	Men	Women	Women as a percentage of total in sex composition category	Men	Women	Women as a percentage of total in sex composition category
0-10	72.8	7.3	3.9	66.6	5.2	3.6	58.7	4.2	4.3
11-20	10.7	4.3	13.9	16.8	5.5	13.6	15.5	3.9	13.6
21-40	5.9	6.3	30.2	5.1	3.9	27.2	11.9	7.4	28.2
41-60	7.1	17.6	50.1	6.5	14.8	52.4	7.0	13.1	54.1
61-80	1.7	11.0	72.3	2.6	12.6	69.5	3.1	10.8	68.7
81-90	0.9	9.5	82.5	1.6	20.2	85.6	3.0	26.6	85.7
91-100	1.0	44.0	94.5	0.7	38.0	96.4	0.8	34.2	96.4
Total[b]	100.0	100.0	28.6	100.0	100.0	32.5	100.0	100.0	38.7
Sample as a percentage of total labor force reporting an occupation	66.1	69.1	–	68.7	68.6	–	67.3	70.1	–

| Index of segregation[c] | 71.9 | 74.1 | 70.7 |

Source: Computed from U.S. Department of Commerce, Bureau of the Census, *U.S. Census of Population: 1960*, Vol. 1, *Characteristics of the Population* pt. 1, U.S. Summary (Washington, D.C.: U.S. Government Printing Office, 1964), Table 201, pp. 522-527; U.S. Department of Commerce, Bureau of the Census, *U.S. Census of the Population, Detailed Characteristics*, Final Report PC(1)-D1, U.S. Summary (Washington, D.C.: U.S. Government Printing Office, 1973), Table 221, pp. 718-724; *Economic Report of the President, 1973* (Washington, D.C.: U.S. Government Printing Office, 1973), Table 33, pp. 155-159.

[a]Based on a sample of 183 detailed census categories.

[b]Rows may not sum to column totals due to rounding.

[c]If x_i is the percentage of the female labor force in the ith sex composition category ($i = 1, \ldots 7$) and y_i is the percentage of the male labor force in the ith sex composition category ($i = 1, \ldots 7$), then the index of segregation is computed as:

$$\frac{\sum_{i=1}^{7} |x_i - y_i|}{2}$$

Table 1-4

Distribution of Men and Women by Sex Composition of Occupational Category in 1950: 1950, 1960, 1970[a]–Experienced Civilian Labor Force, age 14 and over

(Percentages)

Sex composition category (Women as a percentage of total in occupation in 1950)	1950			1960			1970		
	Men	Women	Women as a percentage of total in sex composition category	Men	Women	Women as a percentage of total in sex composition category	Men	Women	Women as a percentage of total in sex composition category
0-10	72.8	7.3	3.9	72.4	6.8	4.4	68.2	7.0	6.1
11-20	10.7	4.3	13.9	11.5	4.5	16.0	12.4	5.4	21.7
21-40	5.9	6.3	30.2	4.8	4.2	30.2	5.9	4.1	30.3
41-60	7.1	17.6	50.1	6.6	17.5	56.4	7.6	17.0	58.5
61-80	1.7	11.0	72.3	2.2	10.7	69.4	2.5	11.4	73.9
81-90	0.9	9.5	82.5	1.2	11.1	83.0	1.6	12.9	84.0
91-100	1.0	44.0	94.5	1.2	45.0	94.5	1.7	42.1	94.0
Total[b]	100.0	100.0	28.6	100.0	100.0	32.5	100.0	100.0	38.7

Source: Computed from U.S. Department of Commerce, Bureau of the Census, *U.S. Census of Population: 1960*, Vol. 1, *Characteristics of the Population*, pt. 1, U.S. Summary (Washington, D.C.: U.S. Government Printing Office, 1964), Table 201, pp. 522-527; U.S. Department of Commerce, Bureau of the Census, *U.S. Census of the Population, Detailed Characteristics*, Final Report PC(1)-D1, U.S. Summary (Washington, D.C.: U.S. Government Printing Office, 1973), Table 221, pp. 718-724; *Economic Report of the President, 1973* (Washington, D.C.: U.S. Government Printing Office, 1973), Table 33, pp. 155-159.

[a]Based on a sample of 183 detailed census categories.

[b]Rows may not sum to column totals due to rounding.

accounted for 4 percent of the men in the sample in 1950 as compared to 2 percent in 1970. Finally, there has been a shift away from self-employment: the proportion of men who were classified as self-employed managers and adminis-trators, n.e.c. (not elsewhere classified), in industry groups where women comprised less than 10 percent of the incumbents in this classification declined from 4 percent in 1950 to 2 percent in 1970 (only those self-employed managers and administrators in n.e.c. categories are reported separately from wage and salary workers in the census occupational listings). While these declines were initially offset by an increase in the proportion of the male work force in other occupations in the 0-10 percent female category (particularly in the operative, professional, and technical groups, and to a lesser extent in craft, managerial, and sales jobs), by 1970 the relative gains in these other categories were outweighed by the continued decline in the farm worker, nonfarm laborer and self-employed classifications.

In contrast to the decline in the proportion of males in the 0-10 percent female category, there was virtually no change in the relative importance of this group of occupations in the female labor force. This sex composition category accounted for roughly 7 percent of women in the sample in all three census years. However, since women were also affected by the declining importance of farm work, nonfarm labor, and self-employment, the fixed representation of women in this sex composition category conceals considerable occupational change.

In 1950, 45 percent of women in the 0-10 percent female group were farm workers, unskilled nonfarm laborers, or in the relevant self-employed manager (n.e.c.) classifications. By 1970 this proportion had fallen to 15 percent. At the same time, the proportion of women in 0-10 percent female occupations who were in operative categories increased from 6 percent to 15 percent, and from 18 percent to 23 percent for women in craft jobs. Smaller but significant increases also occurred (in declining order of importance) in service, sales, clerical, and professional and technical occupations.

Over the twenty-year period there was also an increase in the proportion of both male and female workers in occupations that were 11-20 percent female in 1950. While the increase among males was diffused throughout a variety of detailed classifications, that among females was relatively heavily concentrated in sales and clerical jobs, some of which altered dramatically in sex composition during these years. For example, by 1970 women constituted over 30 percent of the workers in the following jobs which were initially in the 11-20 percent sex-composition category: ticket, station, and express agent; postal clerk; bill and account collector; real estate agent and broker; and huckster and peddler. The latter occupation was 79 percent female in 1970.

In the case of predominantly female occupations, Table 1-4 indicates that the proportion of women in occupations which were 91-100 percent female in 1950 increased slightly between 1950 and 1960, and declined thereafter. The changes in the representation of women in this category were the net effect of two conflicting trends.

On the one hand, there was an increase in the proportion of women in such predominantly female clerical occupations as receptionist, stenographer, typist, and secretary. These occupations accounted for 14 percent of women in the sample in 1950, 17 percent in 1960, and 21 percent in 1970. On the other hand, there was a movement of women out of private household employment, occurring primarily between 1960 and 1970. The proportion of women in detailed occupations in this category was 13 percent in 1950, 12 percent in 1960, and 5 percent in 1970. These opposite movements produced the observed increase in the first ten years of the period and the subsequent decline during the second decade.

The rise in the representation of women in the 81-90 percent female category, shown in Table 1-4, is also strongly related to increases in the proportion of women working in clerical occupations, including those of cashier, file clerk, and office machine operator.

With respect to male employment in predominantly female jobs, Table 1-4 reveals that there was a larger net inflow of men into female categories than of women into male categories. Between 1950 and 1970, the proportion of the male labor force in occupations that were over 60 percent female in 1950 rose by 2.2 percentage points. For the most part this was the result of an increase in the participation of men in such predominantly female professions as elementary school teaching, librarianship, nursing, and social work. There was also an increase in the proportion of men engaged in some of the predominantly female clerical occupations. These gains more than counterbalanced the decline during the same period in the number of men working in private household occupations.

Summary

We find a substantial amount of sex segregation by occupation in all three census years. Both the relative stability in the magnitude of interoccupational segregation and the small changes that have occurred between 1950 and 1970 appear explicable in terms of shifts in the structure of the economy. The declining relative importance of agricultural work, unskilled labor, and self-employment induced a movement of male workers out of occupations which were 0-10 percent female in 1950. At the same time, the rapid expansion of many predominantly female jobs, particularly in the clerical category, permitted the absorption of increasing numbers of women into the labor force without necessitating a greater diffusion of women into predominantly male or integrated job categories. This is not to say that the potential for greater integration was not present during this period. However, given the growth of opportunities in largely female occupations, the absence of greater diversification is at least comprehensible. (Demand conditions in female occupations may not continue to expand as favorably during the 1970s; Hedges 1970, pp. 19-29.)

It is not within the scope of this study to evaluate the relative importance of factors on the demand side (including discrimination) and factors on the supply side in producing sex segregation by occupation. However, the data presented in this section serve to indicate the large differences in the employment distribution among occupations of men and women. These general differences in occupational distribution by sex form the backdrop against which the process of segregation by establishment can be explored. They reveal a situation in which, even in the absence of sex segregation by establishment within occupations, the existence of the predominantly single-sex occupational work group at the enterprise level would be the norm. In this context, intraoccupational segregation may be seen as an additional factor in producing occupational specialization by sex within the firm.

Plan of the Book

The analysis presented here is based on the assumption that there are important institutional and market constraints on the employer's ability to differentiate between male and female labor, and that such limitations must be taken explicitly into account. In Chapter 2 we consider the theoretical concepts and empirical evidence which underlie this view. In Chapter 3 we present a model which predicts the existence of intraoccupational, establishment, and industry segregation, and explains the relationships of such segregation to pay differences between male and female workers. In Chapter 4 we test the hypotheses generated by the model for the employment and wage patterns of male and female workers when occupations are considered separately. In Chapter 5 we test the hypotheses generated by this model when occupations are considered jointly to form a picture of establishment employment and wage patterns. In Chapter 6 the findings of the study are summarized and proposals for labor market policy are presented.

2   The Constraints

The role of employer preferences is frequently given a central place in analyses of discrimination in the labor market, as, for example, in Becker's analysis (1957). However, such models generally proceed from an assumption of perfect competition in the labor market. It is our view that the role of employer preferences can best be understood within the framework of a model that takes explicit account of both the institutional and market constraints under which employers operate. In formulating this model we draw heavily on a theoretical and empirical literature that has dealt much more with production workers than with office workers. Thus the empirical verification of the model will constitute a test of the applicability to nonmanagerial office workers of a model derived from such sources as well as a test of the usefulness of such an approach in analyzing employment segregation and pay differentials between male and female workers.

The constraints on employer behavior that are perceived to be relevant fall into two categories. First are institutional considerations internal to the firm that place limits on the employer's ability to differentiate among individual workers (and thus between male and female workers), particularly with respect to the wage rates paid to men and women within occupational categories and to wage relationships among occupations within the establishment. Second are institutional and market considerations that determine the location of the firm within the wage structure of the local labor market. The position of the firm in the wage hierarchy is seen as having important implications for the employer's ability to recruit male and female labor. In this chapter the theoretical concepts and empirical evidence that underlie the model are summarized.

Intrafirm Constraints: The Internal Labor Market Analysis

The concepts embodied in our model of the intrafirm constraints upon an employer's behavior derive from the notion of an internal labor market,[1] which posits that the job structure of the firm consists of two categories of occupations. First are job categories that are filled from sources external to the firm through the recruitment of new workers. Within clusters of related occupations such jobs, termed *ports of entry*, are generally restricted to lower level positions. Second are job categories that are filled from internal sources through the promotion and upgrading of presently employed workers. Access to

21

such positions usually occurs through advancement up well-defined promotion ladders. The process by which workers advance from entry level positions to higher level jobs is conceptualized as one in which they acquire, either formally or informally, added knowledge or skills that, for the most part, are specific to the firm.

Within this framework the market forces delineated by neoclassical economic analysis are perceived as operating directly on occupations at the entry level. On the other hand, the requirement of enterprise-specific skills for the performance of internally allocated jobs works to prevent the development of a competitive market (in the traditional sense) for these categories of occupations and widens the range of administrative influence within the firm. An internal labor market develops, that is, an administrative apparatus that allocates labor and determines wage rates within the firm.

Employment Stability

A major consequence of the reliance on internal sources of labor is the formation of a relatively permanent attachment between the worker and the firm.

For the employer, the incentive to form a stable employment relationship is based on a desire both to protect the firm's investment in training its employees and to minimize outlays for the recruitment and screening of new workers.[2]

For the employee, two major factors contribute to the maintenance of the employment relationship. First is the widespread practice of filling upper-level positions from internal sources, which implies that access to the firm is often restricted to lower-level entry jobs. Once employees have advanced beyond entry-level positions, they may well be discouraged from making employer changes by the prospect of starting once again at the bottom of a promotion ladder. Second is a network of nontransferable fringe benefits, including pension rights, that provide incentives to workers to remain with their present employer.[3]

The Internal Wage Structure

Since the occupational distribution of the enterprise intersects directly with the market only at entry-level positions, the intrafirm wage determination process will reflect factors not traditionally considered in analyses which focus solely on market forces. For example, job evaluation plans and other formal administrative arrangements are frequently used to specify wage relationships among occupations, as well as base pay rates for each occupational category. Within occupational categories, pay differentials among workers are generally based on seniority and merit considerations.[4] The existence of such formal arrangements makes changes in wage relationships among occupational categories difficult unless they are accompanied by specific alterations in job content. In this regard it is important to note that the rigidity of the specified wage relationships does not derive solely from their simple existence on paper. When the work force is composed of a significant proportion of long-term employees, the effect of custom becomes an additional factor in the stability of interoccupational wage relationships. Thus the occupational pay rankings embodied in the internal wage structure may be expected to be quite rigid even in the absence of codified wage-setting procedures. As Doeringer and Piore state:

Any wage rate, set of wage relationships, or wage setting procedure which prevails over a period of time tends to become customary; changes are then viewed as unjust or inequitable, and the work group will exert economic pressure in opposition to them . . . [In] the modern industrial economy . . . custom tends to grow up around wage *relationships* rather than specific wage *rates* (1971, p. 85).[5]

While it is argued that the existence of an internal labor market within the firm tends to produce a relatively rigid occupational wage structure, it is important to note that such rigidity need not be inconsistent with profit maximization on the part of the firm. For example, it is understandable, especially in firms where workers are not easily replaceable, that employers be concerned about employee morale and its impact on labor productivity. Worker morale may in turn be dependent on the willingness of management to adhere to the customs and traditions of the work place. Thus, from the employee point of view, the legitimacy of the wage determination process depends on management's following the "rules of the game," in this case the specified wage-setting procedures.[6]

Constraints on Employer Behavior

The internal wage structure specifies a set of wage relationships within the firm that are defined primarily in terms of job categories. Wage relationships among individuals, for the most part, are established as a consequence of their job assignment. In this context it is necessary to consider the latitude that the employer possesses to differentiate among individuals.

The employer's latitude appears to be broadest with respect to the selection of new workers for entry jobs and the allocation of workers to job categories filled from internal sources. It is narrowest with respect to wage differentiation among individuals within the same job (such differentials must stay within the bounds determined by seniority and merit considerations) and the alteration of wage relationships among occupational categories.

The possibilities for differentiation among individuals clearly bear upon those for differentiation among workers on the basis of sex. It is expected that the employer would have considerable flexibility in differentiating between men and women in hiring and in the allocation of work. Women may be denied access to certain entry-level positions and thus to their associated promotion ladders (see, for example, the Equal Employment Opportunity Commission 1972, pp. 1243-72). It is also possible that, having gained access to entry-level positions, women may be promoted and upgraded more slowly than male workers. Further, the sex of the majority of the incumbents in an occupational category may have an impact on the design of job structures. For example, predominantly female occupations may be characterized by fewer possibilities for promotion and more numerous ports of entry than comparable male jobs (see, for instance, Smith, pp. 26-27). Again, opportunities may exist at times for reorganizing work and thus for relabeling or redefining specific jobs to permit the recruitment of women at lower rates of pay. Smith reports instances of technological change and work reorganization leading to the entry of women into previously male occupations; however, she presents no evidence regarding the impact on pay rates (Smith, p. 24).

Depending on the extent to which such practices exist, they may have important implications for the segregation of men and women by occupation, as well as for segregation by establishment within occupational categories. Consideration of the range of possibilities is helpful in placing this study in proper perspective.

With respect to differences in the distribution of male and female employment, we are concerned with only one of many possible dimensions of differential treatment, namely, differences in the representation of women in specific occupational categories among firms, taking as given the average representation of women in each occupational category within the local labor market. Thus the implications of the internal labor market analysis for segregation by occupation remain a prime area for future research.

With respect to intraoccupational pay differentials by sex within the firm, our analysis suggests that relatively little scope for differentiation on the basis of sex per se exists. From the industrial-relations point of view, different pay rates by sex for the same job may cause administrative difficulties and foment tensions among workers. Adherence to formal occupational pay structures, including job evaluation plans and other administrative arrangements, is inconsistent with differential pay rates based solely on sex within occupational categories. Moreover, despite some social acceptance of pay differentials based on sex, it may be argued that wage differences that are obviously not based on productivity considerations may undermine in the eyes of workers the legitimacy of the whole wage determination process. An additional consideration of some importance is that the Equal Pay Act of 1963 prohibits differential rates of pay for men and women who perform substantially equal work. These arguments may be weaker in the case of managerial and professional occupations. First, what we may term *individual pay rates* are more frequently established in these categories than in production, clerical, and technical jobs. Second managerial and professional workers were excluded from the coverage of the Equal Pay Act until 1972. However, for the professional occupations in our sample, we do find a pattern of small intrafirm differentials by sex.

Thus, in general, we expect intrafirm pay differentials by sex within occupational categories to reflect only the relatively objective factors of seniority and merit. While we shall proceed under this assumption, two cautions must be borne in mind. First, nominal differences in job titles within the firm may be used to conceal unequal pay for equal work. (The occupational classifications used in this study derive from the allocation of workers to occupation-skill class groups by outside investigators based on an assessment of job content, and thus should include all workers performing similar work, regardless of occupational title.) Indeed, considerable litigation under the Equal Pay Act has revolved around the question of what constitutes substantially equal work (see, for example, Dean 1971, pp. 28-31). Second, although we have no evidence about this matter, it is possible that merit determinations often entailing subjective judgments could in instances be applied in a discriminatory fashion to female workers.

The Interfirm Wage Hierarchy

The wage position of the establishment in comparison to other firms in the local labor market would clearly be a factor of some importance in recruiting labor. Local labor market studies generally indicate considerable wage dispersion of firms.[7] The causes of wage differences among firms are exceedingly complex and appear to represent the cumulative effect of a variety of factors. Moreover, these factors are highly interrelated and may vary in relative importance and impact at different points in time, as well as among different types of enterprises and labor markets. Since the primary focus of this study is upon sex differences in earnings and employment, we do not endeavor to construct a unified theory of interfirm wage dispersion. Rather, the factors that tend to cause wage differences among firms are reviewed, with particular attention given to the reasons why individuals may be expected to receive differential rates of pay depending on the establishment of employment.

Worker Quality: Exogenously Determined

One possible explanation for interfirm pay differentials is that they reflect interfirm differences in worker quality. Such an explanation implies that costs per efficiency unit of labor are in fact equal among firms, thus making the observed establishment variation in wage rates more compatible with competitive models. If one were to argue further that worker quality is exogenously determined by the individual characteristics of workers, then establishment of employment could not be considered a causal factor in pay differences among individuals. Indeed the only remaining question of interest would be why some firms maximize profits by hiring or retaining lower quality workers at lower wages, while others do so by hiring or retaining higher quality workers at higher wages. (This view may be further expanded to allow for pay differences based on the nonpecuniary advantages and disadvantages of employment in different firms.)

It is our view that exogenously determined worker quality may well be an element in interfirm wage differences; however, it is not the sole explanatory factor. Interfirm pay differentials in excess of exogenously determined worker quality are the result of at least two sets of factors. First is the joint determination by establishment as well as individual characteristics of worker quality and other elements of labor cost (e.g., turnover rates). Such interfirm wage differences may well be cost equalizing, although a reallocation of workers among firms could still alter the wage outcomes (and productivities) of individual workers. Second are institutional and market factors that allow pay differences in excess of labor costs to persist.

Establishment Characteristics and Labor Quality

The internal labor market analysis suggests that a range of alternatives is open to the firm in terms of hiring practices, work organization, and wage policies. These alternatives may be illustrated by the dichotomy between *primary* and *secondary* employment elucidated in the dual labor market analysis.[8]

The Dual Labor Market Analysis. The primary market has the characteristics of a highly developed internal labor market. Entry is restricted to relatively few lower-level jobs and promotion ladders are long; worker stability is encouraged by high wages, opportunities for advancement, good working conditions, and provisions for job security. The administration of work rules is characterized by adherence to the principles of equity and due process.

The secondary market more closely approximates what have been termed *unstructured markets.* The occupational distribution is characterized by numerous ports of entry, and promotion ladders are short or nonexistent; worker stability is discouraged by low wages, little opportunity for advancement, and often poor working conditions and little provision for job security. The administration of work rules may be characterized by arbitrary and even harsh discipline.

The desired long-term attachment between workers and firms leads employers in primary-sector establishments to place great weight on the future performance prospects of new workers, and particularly on their potential for job stability. Groups of workers viewed by employers as having unstable work patterns may be excluded for employment in the primary sector. However, we believe that many of the individuals who are so excluded do possess the requisite behavioral characteristics for primary-sector employment. While productivity or labor cost differences or both may account for a significant portion of the wage differences between such individuals and those employed in the primary sector, they would reflect the way in which the work is structured in the establishment rather than the characteristics of workers.

Additional Applications of the Internal Labor Market Analysis. It is argued that the distinction between the primary and secondary sectors is not technologically determinate, that is, that the work performed in a significant portion of jobs may be organized in either of the two fashions (Piore 1971, p. 92). This raises a host of additional possibilities for fine gradations among a variety of job characteristics beyond the primary-secondary dichotomy. (For a study of the relationships between establishment wage rates, search costs, and training costs see Ullman, (1968), pp. 153-65. Ullman's thesis is that some of the interfirm pay differences may be explained by differences among firms in training costs, for which experience and training variables are a proxy, and search costs. Stated somewhat differently, Ullman argues that due to the impact of these factors interfirm wage differences overstate actual differences in labor costs. However, he finds that the measured effect of training and search costs is not of a sufficient magnitude to account for the major part of the wage differences. Thus it would appear that differences in labor costs remain a factor in interfirm pay differences.) Further, it points to the possibility of joint determination of worker quality by both worker characteristics and establishment practices.

Thus, for example, the magnitude of labor turnover may perhaps be seen in part as the reflection of the personal characteristics of workers, but it is also related to the wage rate paid by the firm, the opportunities offered for advancement, working conditions, and the quality of management.[9] Similarly, the skill levels of employees may reasonably be related to the existence and quality of training programs or training opportunities and the diligence and effort expended by workers in job-related tasks to the wage standing of the firm and various personnel practices.[10] These considerations are well summarized by Richard Lester: "In the long run, the effectiveness of a firm's work force may be influenced much more by the development of people under the management's supervision and personnel operations than it is by the apparent quality of new recruits at the time of their initial employment" (Lester 1954, p. 31).

Thus it appears that an establishment's wage and personnel practices have an important impact on the quality of its labor force as measured by turnover rates, skill acquired through firm-specific training, and effort and attention paid to job-related tasks. For some workers, denial of access to higher-wage establishments may mean not only that they receive lower wages, but also that they are less productive in the jobs they do secure. Although establishment pay differentials may be offset by differences in labor costs, the latter are not altogether determined by the individual characteristics of workers.

The Overcrowding Hypothesis. A similar argument has been made by proponents of the "overcrowding hypothesis" (Bergmann 1974). The overcrowding hypothesis has been developed to account for the case in which perfectly substitutable male and female (or white and black) labor is segregated into two occupations. Here we apply it to the case of segregation by firm within occupations. Bergmann argues that employer discrimination of an exclusionary nature generates an overcrowding in the female sector. An important point in her analysis is that employers who do hire women will utilize the labor-intensive production techniques that their lower wages make profitable. Thus it is possible for potentially equally productive female labor to receive lower wages than male labor, and yet still receive its marginal product. The capital-to-labor ratio, which would not be related to wage rates under perfectly competitive conditions, will be associated with wage differences when the labor market is segmented. As in the internal labor market analysis, productivity differences derive from establishment rather than solely from individual differences.

Interfirm Wage Differences in Excess of Labor Costs

As noted earlier institutional and market factors that allow interfirm wage differentials in excess of labor costs to persist are related to interfirm pay differences in excess of labor quality. Such factors include barriers to worker mobility and information, employer hiring practices, and structural factors including degree of competitiveness in product markets and the impact of unionization.

Barriers to Worker Mobility and Information. Perhaps most obviously suggested by the internal labor market analysis to explain interfirm pay differences is the reduction of labor mobility implied by the frequent restriction of job openings to lower-level entry positions and the existence of nontransferable fringe benefits. As a result of these factors, workers in higher-level positions are, to some extent, insulated from external competition. Kerr argues that such insulation from outside competition is introduced into labor markets even in the absence of institutional rules: ". . . workers and employers form attachments for each other which neither like to break lightly . . . and separation is for cause only. Thus most jobs, even without institutional rules, belong to single workers or to small groups of workers . . . Institutional rules, however, add new rights and new preferences and strengthen the old ties" (1954, pp. 95-96). A related consideration is that the existence of highly developed internal labor markets greatly increases the amount of information essential for workers to make rational selections among firms. Information is needed not only about entry pay rates, but also about promotion prospects and the incremental earnings associated with progression up promotion ladders. Job security, fringe benefit levels, and working conditions must be taken into account as well by prospective employees. The possibility of their making decisions based on incomplete information is great. Lester reports that upon completion of an intensive study of the Trenton labor market ". . . the investigators, armed with all of the knowledge gained from the interviews and plant inspections, were themselves stumped to decide which one, or half dozen, among 82 companies they themselves would select to apply for employment. The unknown factors and future uncertainties were so great as to frustrate an attempt at calculation and rational choice (1954, p. 48). In light of barriers to mobility and to complete information, it is understandable that pay differences among firms may develop and persist at a level in excess of what may reasonably be attributed to quality differences among workers or to the equalization of the net advantages of alternative employments. Even when worker mobility among firms is reduced by institutional factors, workers' discontentment with their level of remuneration could affect morale and thus productivity. However, some evidence (Reynolds 1951, pp. 157-58) suggests that wage differences among firms tend over time to become recognized and customary. Thus to avoid morale problems management need only protect the firm's relative position in the wage hierarchy rather than endeavor to achieve absolute equality with other firms.

Employer Hiring Practices. Since the recruitment and selection of new workers is a major area of employer discretion, it is important to consider the hiring practices of employers in relation to the quality of workers hired, and the implications for differences in worker quality among firms. The screening of job applicants inevitably entails some subjective judgments as well as considerable uncertainty, and the existence of internal labor markets enhances the elements of uncertainty. In addition to an assessment of the applicant's probable performance in entry-level positions, consideration must also be given to the individual's "trainability" and probable future performance in the higher-level positions along associated promotion ladders. Where turnover is costly, employers' preferred hiring standards may reflect a greater concern with avoiding the costs associated with the selection of an unqualified applicant than with preventing the rejection of a qualified individual. Doeringer and Piore (1971, pp. 103-104) deal with this subject. These concerns, combined with the subjective elements in hiring decisions, suggest that preferred or ideal hiring standards may often be too restrictive, operating to exclude individuals who are capable of performing well. These arguments are well stated by Doeringer and Piore:

Screening is almost always probabilistic. The variables upon which it is based are chosen because they correlate or, are believed to correlate, with job performance. Occasionally, the correlation is statistically valid, but most often it derives from the collective experience and prejudices of the plant management and has never been scientifically verified. In either case, the causal relationship between screening variables and job performance is not necessarily well defined. In fact, only in rare instance are managers able to articulate a plausible relationship between job performance and the screening procedures they employ (1971, p. 103).

Of importance for the study of male-female employment differences in the present context is the postulated existence of what Piore has termed *statistical discrimination*, wherein individual members of a group that is viewed by employers as less stable *on the average* are excluded from certain types of employment on a probabilistic basis (1971, p. 91). An assessment of probabilities may remain foremost in the employer's mind, even when his own experience indicates that individual women, for example, can become long-term employees. One employer surveyed in a local labor market study stated that if his present payroll supervisor (a woman) were to leave, he would replace her with a man—only because of the greater employment permanency of men. Yet this particular woman had been with the firm for fifteen years (Smith, p. 25). (In citing this view, we are in no way suggesting that it is true. To our knowledge, no evidence exists to support the proposition that, *other things being equal*, women have higher turnover or absenteeism rates.)

Some evidence that applicants in less-preferred categories are capable of performing the jobs from which they are excluded is provided by the tendency of firms to "lower" hiring standards when necessary, as when the labor market generally tightens, or when specific product market conditions are favorable for employment expansion.[11] Such evidence does not, of course, prove that the lowering of hiring standards is without cost to the firm. Documentation does exist, however, of one case (described below) in which such an adjustment appears to have been fairly costless, and indeed, in the view of many employers, to have had distinct advantages.

The large post-World War II expansion in demand for workers in traditionally female jobs, in combination with a variety of demographic factors (e.g., the low birth rates of the 1930s), produced a shortage in the supply of young, single women who had been the preferred group of female workers in the pre-1940 period. As a result, employers were increasingly forced to hire older, married women, and contrary to expectation, often found that they were, in fact, more stable and dependable workers than young, single women (Oppenheimer 1970, pp. 127-39).

Given the probabilistic nature of the screening process, as well as the, in many cases, relatively tenuous relationship between screening criteria and job performance, there is a high probability that the screening process will exclude some individuals as capable as those hired. In addition, in view of the possibility of statistical discrimination and of discrimination "pure and simple" (Piore 1971, p. 91) or Becker-type discrimination (Becker 1957) against women and other groups, this probability appears even greater.

A consideration of employer hiring practices is of importance to an analysis of the relationship between the wage position of the firm and the quality of labor the firm is able to recruit. It appears likely that higher-wage firms are able to adopt more restrictive hiring standards than lower-wage establishments.[12] However, it also appears likely from the preceding discussion that restrictive hiring standards will result in the rejection of some equally qualified individuals, who will thus be forced to seek employment in lower-paying establishments. Consequently there will not necessarily be a one-to-one relationship between the wage standing of the firm and the quality of new employees. Of course, in considering the actual performance of workers on the job, we also need to take into account the impact of establishment characteristics on worker quality as discussed earlier.

Structural Factors. Considerable evidence exists that structural elements are important in creating pay differentials among firms. Among the characteristics of the establishment that have been hypothesized to be significantly related to wage rates are type of industry (especially in regard to differences in the degree of competition and profit rates among industries), size of firm, and extent of unionization.[13]

It is often difficult to distinguish empirically the pure effect of such structural factors on pay differences. For example, while Weiss found the degree of concentration and unionization to be positively related to wage differences among industries, some of the differential was explained by such indicators of worker quality as educational attainment. In addition, he found that high-wage industries employed a relatively high proportion of "preferred" groups of workers (whites as opposed to blacks, and males as opposed to females) (1966).

Weiss's findings imply that the high-wage industries "get their money's worth," either through imposing higher quality standards or by indulging their preferences for particular groups of workers. Ashenfelter and Johnson (1972, pp. 488-509) argue that wage rates, unionization, and worker quality should be viewed as jointly determined. Using two-stage least squares to estimate such a model, they find the impact of unionization is substantially reduced. However, their study is limited to an extremely small sample of industries. Moreover, in our view it is seriously misspecified because percent female in the industry is considered an exogenous variable. Further, while the authors imply that firms make quality adjustments around a union rate, their empirical evidence sheds no light on this question, since, in their model, worker quality (represented by educational attainment) is completely determined by exogenous variables (skill mix and urbanization). Similarly, the often-observed positive effect of size of firm on wage rates may reflect a host of factors ranging from market power to differential average worker quality between large and small firms.[14] In light of the interdependency between establishment and worker characteristics in the determination of labor quality, it is particularly difficult to determine the extent to which the wage differentials associated with such structural factors are cost-equalizing. The range of interdependency may even extend to the speed of technological progress. Slichter has argued that "the strong pressure of unions for higher wages ... has undoubtedly helped to raise the standard of living because this pressure has forced management to work harder to keep down labor costs and has thereby accelerated technological progress" (1951, p. 13). However, the important question for our purposes is whether individuals will be differentially rewarded depending on the establishment of employment (and, in this case, on the industry, union status, and size of the firm), and not whether such wage differences are cost-equalizing.

Empirical Evidence: Pay Differentials and
Individual Characteristics

The determination of the impact of individual characteristics on earnings is plagued by two opposing problems. On the one hand, as we have emphasized, many of the characteristics associated with individuals may be at least partially determined by establishment wage and personnel practices. (When the possibility of economy-wide discrimination is taken into account, the exogenous nature of almost any individual characteristic may be open to question. Madden (1973, p. 2) defines "cumulative discrimination" as occurring when a factor has a lower level of productivity due to past discrimination.) On the other hand, many of the individual characteristics that are associated with productivity, such as ability and motivation, are not easily subject to measurement. However, despite these difficulties, it seems reasonable to consider a general finding that pay differences among establishments (or groups of establishments categorized by industry, union status, or size of firm) exceed what may be attributed to the individual characteristics of workers (as determined by such factors as occupation, education, age, and experience) as evidence of differential wage outcomes depending on the establishment of employment.[15]

Eaton Conant examined the relationship between the aptitude test scores and starting salaries of female high school graduates who had been placed as typists by the state employment service in Madison, Wisconsin (1963). Although Conant found a statistically significant difference between the test scores of women hired by employers in the top third of the salary range and those hired by employers in the bottom third, the average quality differential accounted for only 10 percent of the difference in starting salaries. A similar finding is reported by Joseph Ullman who explored interfirm differences in pay rates for typists and keypunch operators in the Chicago labor market (1968). He found that the several measures of experience and training of individual workers that he used only partially explained wage differences.

In their intensive study of a variety of blue- and white-collar occupations in the Chicago labor market, Albert Rees and George Schultz also found that differences in the individual characteristics of workers provided only a partial explanation of earnings differences. (This study is particularly noteworthy for the richness of data obtained on worker characteristics.) Furthermore, the authors suggest that these differences may be related to establishment characteristics. While uneven results were obtained for the impact of a number of specific establishment variables on wage rates, the authors point out that "it remains likely that there are more consistent patterns of establishment characteristics in the Chicago labor market than we have reported, and that we have missed them because we sampled too few establishments (1970, p. 189). (The authors also note some multicolinearity problems in disentangling the impact of certain individual and establishment variables. This is not surprising, especially in a relatively small sample, given the probability that some part of the interfirm differences in pay rates is due to differences in worker quality. Wachtel and Betsey (1972, pp. 121-29) provide a fuller discussion of the multicolinearity problem.) Ronald Oaxaca, (1973) using a larger sample of individuals from the 1967 Survey of Economic Opportunity found that, after controlling for the personal characteristics of workers and their major occupational group, the industry type and the union status of the individual were important variables for explaining the wage rates of both men and women.

While the magnitude of the pay differential that is due solely to establishment of employment may be difficult to ascertain, it seems reasonable on the basis of both theoretical considerations and available evidence to assume that this factor does generate pay differences among workers with similar productivity-related characteristics. (Bluestone, Murphy, and Stevenson (1973, pp. 167-225) offer further documentation of this point.)

Conclusion

The analytical framework employed in this study takes explicit account of the institutional and market constraints under which employers operate. In this chapter, the theoretical concepts and empirical evidence that underlie this approach were summarized. In the next chapter, a model that incorporates these constraints is presented.

The internal labor market analysis was drawn upon to identify two important institutional constraints operating within the firm. First, the employer is seen as being constrained to offer the same base pay rates to all incumbents of an occupational category, regardless of sex. Pay differentiation among individuals in the same job category must remain within the relatively narrow bounds of seniority and merit considerations. Second, the employer is seen as facing a relatively rigid occupational wage structure that specifies wage relationships among occupational categories.

In addition, the ability of the firm to recruit labor is seen as being dependent upon the wage position of the establishment in comparison to other firms in the local labor market. The existence of a hierarchy of firms with respect to wage rates within the local labor market may be seen to result from the interplay of a variety of factors ranging from institutional considerations (such as establishment hiring and other personnel practices) to market forces (such as the degree of competition in the product market). While interfirm pay differences may result in part from differences in the average quality of labor among firms, the relationship is a complex one, since establishment policies influence both labor turnover rates and worker productivity. We have argued that pay differences among firms are generally in excess of what may be attributed to exogenously determined worker quality. In our view, this argument finds considerable theoretical support and is consistent with a large body of empirical evidence.

The factors involved in interfirm pay differences suggest that worker stability is likely to be an important factor governing access to higher-wage establishments. Thus if women are viewed by employers, correctly or incorrectly, as being on the average less stable workers than men (i.e., as having higher rates of turnover and absenteeism), then individual women may be excluded from certain types of employment on a probabilistic basis. In addition, since higher-wage firms tend to be shielded to some extent from competitive forces, women are more likely to face Becker-type discrimination or discrimination "pure and simple" on the part of these firms.

3   The Model

In this chapter a model is presented for analyzing the existence of intraoccupational, establishment, and industry segregation and for explaining their relationship to wage differences between male and female workers. This model assumes that employers exercise their hiring preferences regarding the sex of workers within the market and institutional constraints that were reviewed in Chapter 2. The implications of this model are then contrasted with those of two alternative models that have been proposed by Gary Becker, of employer and employee discrimination.

The Model

For the analysis to be developed in this section, the most important constraints on employer behavior are assumed to be the following:

1. Within firms, uniform base pay rates are established for each occupational category, regardless of sex. Variation in rates of remuneration paid to individual workers within the same occupational category can only reflect differences in seniority and merit (ability). (Sex segregation by occupation or within occupations by firm, or both, may result in single-sex establishment work forces within specific occupational categories. This constraint is still operative in these cases in the sense that the firm would have to pay a new worker of the opposite sex, whether recruited from internal or external sources, the same occupational pay rate as presently employed workers receive.)
2. Within the firm, relative wage structures are rigid (i.e., wage relationships among occupational categories tend to be relatively inflexible).
3. Market forces and institutional factors determine a hierarchy of firms with respect to entry wage rates. The constraints postulated in (1) and (2) imply that the wage standing of the firm is consistent across related occupations and across sex groups.[1]

These three constraints operate on the demand side to yield a structure of occupational wage rates which may be offered by the firm, regardless of the sex of the worker employed. As our discussion in Chapter 2 suggests, the resulting wage structure has been shaped by a variety of factors, and cannot easily be

35

adjusted simply to accommodate employer preferences regarding the sex composition of establishment employment. Thus, in considering the relationship between the wage rate and the sex composition of employment, the position of the firm in the wage hierarchy is taken to be predetermined.

It is argued that the wage rates offered by the higher-wage establishments in each occupational category are in excess of what would be needed to attract a sufficient supply of labor, that is, the wage rate offered is in excess of the wage rate that would be determined by the interaction of supply and demand. One of the advantages of a high-wage position is that it provides the employer with the opportunity to pick and choose from workers in a relatively large labor pool. In this situation, jobs are rationed not by the price mechanism but rather by employer hiring preferences.[2] The higher the wage ranking of the firm, the greater the employer's freedom to exercise preferences. As we progress down the wage hierarchy, this latitude is diminished, and towards the bottom of the hierarchy the firm may simply have to take what it can get. In addition, as we progress down the wage hierarchy supply considerations become more important in determining the establishment wage rate. If an adequate supply of labor is not forthcoming at the wage rate offered by the low-wage firm, some wage adjustment will be necessary. In contrast, the high-wage employer has the option of either turning to a less preferred group of workers or adjusting the wage rate. This view is consistent with the finding that the interindustry wage structure narrows during upswings in the business cycle, as low-wage firms find it necessary to improve their relative wage position in order to maintain an adequate supply of labor. In contrast, high-wage firms which normally face an excess supply of labor are under considerably less pressure. Wachter (1970) offers evidence of the cyclical compression of the interindustry wage structure.

It is argued that in sexually mixed occupations there exists a fairly widespread preference among employers for male over female labor. A preference for male labor could be based on a broad spectrum of attitudes ranging from simple distaste for employing women, particularly outside a narrow group of traditionally female occupations, to employer beliefs about the differences in the quality of or costs associated with male and female labor. Such reasons would not be directly relevant to our argument unless they were correctly based on factors which affect labor costs. An additional possibility is that employers themselves are indifferent to the sex of the worker hired, but that male employees have preferences against working with women. Employers might then give some weight to this consideration. However, as we shall see, a model in which all discriminatory tastes are located in employees produces very different outcomes than would be predicted by our model.

While the preference for male labor is expected to be fairly widespread, the ability to exercise this preference is not. In general, the higher-wage employers will be freer to indulge whatever preferences they have for hiring men, and we expect in general that they will do so. (In addition, as the discussion in Chapter

2 indicates, higher-wage firms are more likely to invest heavily in their work forces and thus to put a premium on job stability. This implies that women are more likely to face statistical discrimination on the part of these firms. Moreover, to the extent that higher-wage firms are insulated from competitive forces in their product markets, women are more likely to experience Becker-type discrimination on the part of such firms.) The lower the wage offered by the firm, the less able the establishment will be to compete with the high-wage firms for male labor. This difficulty may be reflected to some extent in higher costs since prolonged search may be necessary to locate male workers and, once they have been hired, it may be more difficult to retain them since they may be attracted by more lucrative opportunities elsewhere. Since, due to segregation by occupation, the proportion which men comprise of total occupational employ-ment differs among job categories, the representation of men is expected to differ among job categories in the firm. However, after controlling for the occupational mix of the establishment and thus the differing availability of male labor among job categories, we expect that men will comprise a higher proportion of the work force in firms which pay higher wages to both men and women, while women will be more highly represented in firms which pay lower wages to workers of both sexes.

Let us consider the implications of the model at the level of the occupation-al category. We distinguish three types of firms with respect to the sex composition of occupational employment: firms that hire only men, firms that hire both men and women, and firms that hire only women. We visualize a ranking of firms with respect to wage rates offered. High-wage firms for the most part hire male workers. As they occupy progressively lower positions in the wage hierarchy, firms are forced to turn increasingly to female labor so that finally the lowest-wage firms have completely female occupational work forces. (The size of the three sectors—male, female and mixed—will vary with the relative availability of men and women in each occupational category. In occupations in which women comprise a very high proportion of total employment the male and integrated sectors will be very small.) Differences in individual employer preferences, which may also differ somewhat by occupational category, may alter this result in specific cases, but this is expected to be the general pattern. Since, in this view, the sex composition of the establishment's occupational work force is determined by the position of the firm in the wage hierarchy in combination with employer hiring preferences, and not by random factors, sex segregation by firm (intraoccupational segregation) is expected to exist. Thus the model yields a prediction regarding the distribution of male and female workers among firms within occupational categories.

The model also yields predictions regarding male and female wage rates. First, it is hypothesized that within firms men and women receive the same base occupational pay rate. Thus the model predicts that, within occupational categories, intrafirm pay differentials by sex will be small relative to the average market-wide occupational pay differential between men and women. Second, establishments that are completely segregated within an occupational category will tend to represent the extremes of the occupational wage distribution. Thus it is expected that there will be a relationship between the average wages of each sex group and the sex composition of establishment employment. Specifically, the average wage of women employed in the firms that employ only women in the occupational category is expected to be less than the average wage of women employed in firms that hire both sexes. Similarly, the average wage of men employed in the men-only firms is expected to be higher than the average wage of men employed by firms that hire both men and women into the occupational category. Third, it is expected that the average market-wide occupational pay differential between men and women will be primarily the result of differences in pay rates among firms rather than of differences in pay rates within firms. This is expected to be the case even when we consider the pay differential by sex among workers employed in firms that hire both sexes into the occupational category, and to be more markedly apparent when we consider the pay differential by sex among all workers employed in the occupational category.

While the model yields working hypotheses regarding employment and wage patterns of workers when occupations are considered separately, the verification of the model also requires that occupations be considered jointly to form a picture of establishment employment and wage patterns. First, we expect to find a wage hierarchy of establishments within the local labor market that is consistent across related occupational categories and across sex groups, that is, that the high-wage firms must pay relatively high wages in all occupational categories and to workers of both sexes. Second, since the representation of women in the establishment is determined by the standing of the firm in the wage hierarchy in combination with employer hiring preferences, we would expect to find establishment segregation. In other words, we expect significant and consistent differences to appear among firms in the representation of women in the establishment work force, after controlling for differences in the occupational mix of establishments. Firms which tend to employ a higher-than-expected proportion of women in one occupational category should also do so in other categories, while firms which employ a lower-than-expected proportion of women in one occupational category should also do so in other categories. (We do not expect to find any women-only or men-only establishments when a broad range of occupational categories are included in the analysis. Interoccupational segregation results in some occupational categories that are so overwhelmingly comprised of men and others which are so overwhelmingly comprised of women that male and female workers are bound to be represented to some extent in all firms.) Third, the model predicts that there will be an inverse relationship between the ranking of the establishment with respect to the representation of women and its ranking with respect to wages. The lower the wage standing of the firm, the higher the representation of women, and vice versa. Fourth, when we consider the determinants of the wage ranking of the establishment, it is expected that establishment characteristics that are associated with higher wage rates will also be associated with a lower representation of women, and vice versa. Thus, to the extent that industry type is an important determinant of the wage standing of the establishment, we expect to find evidence of industry segregation.

It has been argued that the major cause of the pay differential by sex within occupational categories is the differential distribution of male and female workers among firms, particularly that resulting from the exclusionary practices of the high-wage firms. However, it may alternatively be argued that if interfirm pay differences are primarily the result of differences in the quality of labor among establishments, these differential wage outcomes would persist even if workers were redistributed among establishments. While the matter is certainly not beyond dispute, it is our view that the interfirm pay differences exceed what would result from differences in the individual productivity-related characteristics of workers and thus that individual wage outcomes would be changed by a redistribution of workers among firms. We now examine the characteristics of our own data which bear on the interpretation of our findings.

While we have no data regarding the personal characteristics of workers other than sex, we are able to classify individuals by narrowly defined occupational categories. Most of the detailed occupational categories are further subdivided into skill classes. While, in empirical work, homogeneity of labor is often approximated by certain personal characteristics of workers (including the human capital they possess through formal schooling and post-school training), ours is a more functional approach to the concept of homogeneity, that is the ability to perform certain specific tasks.[3] We argue that such a functional approach has equal merit. While we concede that quality differences may exist among workers in the same job category and skill class, just as there may be quality differences among workers with equal schooling and experience, such differences are expected to be relatively small. Furthermore, it is expected that variation in individual characteristics among workers, such as training or experience, which do in fact influence productivity will be reflected in the progression through skill grades within an occupation. These factors, in conjunction with the evidence which we have reviewed from other sources, make it reasonable to assume that a significant portion of firm differences in pay rates is the result of factors other than differences in the individual productivity-related characteristics of workers, and thus that a reallocation of workers among establishments could alter wage outcomes for individual workers.[4]

Despite the relative homogeneity of labor within these detailed occupational categories, in the absence of additional information on the personal characteristics of workers we do not attempt to estimate the proportion of the male-female wage differential that is the result of discrimination in specific occupational categories. (We have argued that it is unlikely that exogenously determined differences in worker quality are the sole explanatory factor in interfirm pay differences. However, even if this has been established to the reader's satisfaction, it gives us no guidelines for allocating the differential in specific cases.) Rather, we base the interpretation of our findings and our policy prescriptions on a consistent pattern of association between pay differentials and differences in the distribution of employment of men and women, observed over a large number of occupations. Moreover, we attempt to establish that interfirm pay differences in specific occupational categories are part of a larger pattern of establishment pay differences that are consistent across occupations and sex groups. Furthermore, were high- and low-wage firms randomly scattered throughout industry groups, it would suggest, although not prove, that interfirm wage differences simply reflect differences in labor costs. That is, it would imply that the high-wage firm is able to compete with the low-wage firm in any product market. (Such a finding would not be inconsistent with our argument that a reallocation of workers among firms could change wage outcomes for individual workers, since in our view labor costs are jointly determined by worker and establishment characteristics.) Should our findings indicate that, on the contrary, high- and low-wage firms tend to be located in different industries, it would suggest that labor costs are a factor in interfirm wage differences.

Alternative Models

The model presented in this chapter may be contrasted with two alternative views which have been analyzed by Gary Becker (1957). In the first case, discriminatory tastes are located in employers; in the second case, in employees.

Employer Preferences

We may term this case as one of *unconstrained* employer preferences to differentiate it from our model in which employer preferences play an important role but are subject to the constraints imposed by institutional factors and market forces. In this model, employers who have tastes for discrimination against women workers will hire women only if the wage difference between male and female labor is large enough to compensate for the disutility of employing women. One can postulate a structure of employer preferences that would result in some degree of both intraoccupational and establishment segregation. (Although this would require an extremely skewed distribution of employer tastes.) Industry segregation may also exist; however, it would not in this case be the result of a predetermined structure of wage differentials among industries, but rather to similar preferences among employers within industry groups.

A number of important differences between the two models emerge when we consider the relationship between employment and wage patterns. First, within occupational categories, there would be no significant pay differentials between the women employed in integrated firms and those employed in segregated firms, and the same would apply in the case of male workers. It follows that the wage differential between men and women employed in the same firm would be roughly the same magnitude as the average market-wide sex differential within the occupation. These points follow from the traditional neoclassical view that a market wage rate is determined for both types of labor, and that no firm would pay wages above the market rate (nor could a firm pay less). Equally important, there would be no constraint within the firm that would prevent different pay rates for men and women in the same job (that is, wage flexibility is assumed).

Second, even if we allow for some variation in rates of remuneration for male and female labor depending on the establishment in which they are employed, it would not be predicted that women would constitute a lower proportion of total employment in firms that pay higher wages to both men and women. That is, it is not expected that male and female pay rates will follow the same pattern by establishment of employment. On the contrary, we expect firms that hire a greater-than-expected proportion of male workers to be those firms that prefer men and will hire women only at a lower wage rate.

Third, it is unlikely that establishment characteristics that are associated with higher wages regardless of the sex of the worker will be associated with a lower representation of women in the firm. (Becker does, however, expect that monopolistic industries will be freer to indulge their tastes for discrimination since they are more insulated from the forces of competition. If such industries do pay higher wages to men they may also do so to the women they employ particularly if such female workers are restricted to "acceptable" job categories.)

The Becker model emphasizes that, other things being equal, employer tastes for discrimination result in lower profits. In our model, however, it becomes clear that other things are seldom equal between the firms that tend to discriminate (that is, to exclude women) and the firms that do not. And it may well be that it is the lower-profit firms that do employ women since they can least afford to discriminate. While this observation is not necessarily contrary to the Becker view, it does shed some light on the persistence of discrimination over time. Competitive pressures are strongest within product markets and thus, as noted earlier, would be expected to enforce some homogeneity in wage and employment patterns within industry groupings. However, the forces of competition are weaker across industries, relying for their operation on a mobility of capital and labor among industries. The persistence of interindustry wage differentials over time would indicate that, for a variety of reasons, this factor does not operate with the force that might be expected on purely theoretical grounds.

Employee Preferences

A second case which Becker describes is that of employee discrimination, wherein the tastes for discrimination are located in employees rather than employers. The existence of employee discrimination may have significant effects on the employment of women workers even in the absence of employer discrimination. The major thrust of this factor would be towards segregation—intraoccupational segregation if discriminatory employee tastes were against substitutes, and establishment segregation if they were against complements. Segregation results from the efforts of employers to avoid paying a premium to male workers to induce them to work with female labor. While a distaste on the part of male workers for working with women can produce segregation, it should not result in pay differences.

However, complete segregation may not be possible. In particular, where the firm incurs substantial adjustment costs associated with hiring and firing workers, it is possible that it will not be profitable for the firm to entirely shift the sex composition of its work force in response to a wage differential between men and women (Arrow 1973, p. 22). Also working against the likelihood of complete segregation in the case of complementary labor is the fact that the existence of sex segregation by occupation may make it difficult to form single-sex work units. Where complete segregation is not possible, discriminatory tastes on the part of employees can lead to wage differences combined with tendencies toward segregation (Arrow 1973, p. 23). Under these circumstances, one might observe different rates of remuneration for male labor depending on whether it is employed with female labor. However, the wage implications of this model are quite different from those of our model. In the employee discrimination case it is expected that male workers will be paid a premium when they work with women and thus be more highly remunerated than when they work with men.

Conclusion

In this chapter we have developed a model explaining the relationship of intraoccupational, establishment, and industry segregation to wage differences between male and female workers. This model yields hypotheses amenable to empirical testing when occupational categories are considered both separately and jointly. The following hypotheses have been identified:

1. At the level of the occupational category
   a. There will exist intraoccupational segregation.
   b. The average wage of women employed in women-only firms will be less than the average wage of women employed in integrated firms, while

the average wage of men employed in the segregated firms will be above the average wage of men employed in integrated firms.

c. When both men and women are employed in the same firm, intrafirm pay differentials by sex will be small relative to market-wide occupational pay differences.

d. Market-wide occupational pay differentials by sex will be the result primarily of differences in pay rates among firms rather than of differences in pay rates within firms.

2. At the level of the establishment

a. There will exist establishment segregation.

b. There will exist an establishment wage hierarchy.

c. There will be an inverse relationship between the relative ranking of the establishment with respect to the representation of women and its ranking with respect to wages.

d. Establishment characteristics that are positively related to wage rates will be negatively related to the representation of women in the establishments, and vice versa.

e. To the extent that industry is an important factor in interfirm wage differences, we expect to find industry segregation.

In Chapter 4, we test the hypotheses regarding sex differences in wage rates and employment distributions within occupational categories. In general, the results confirm our expectations of finding strong evidence of intraoccupational segregation. In most cases, women employed in firms that hire only women into the occupational category earn less on the average than those employed in firms that employ both sexes, while men in male-only firms tend to earn more than do men in integrated establishments. Intrafirm pay differentials by sex are shown on the average to be small relative to market-wide occupational pay differences. Because of both the high level of intraoccupational segregation and the relatively small magnitude of intrafirm pay differences, pay differences among firms account for a high proportion of market-wide occupational pay differentials by sex.

In Chapter 5, we further test the model by examining establishment wage and employment patterns. After controlling for the effects of occupation mix and sex composition of establishment employment, we demonstrate the existence of a wage hierarchy of establishments that is consistent across occupations and sex groups. We show that establishment segregation does exist: after controlling for the occupation mix of the firm and thus the differential availability of women in each occupational category, we find that establishments exhibit consistent patterns with respect to the utilization of women across occupational categories. Further, the ranking of establishments with respect to the representation of women in the firm is inversely related to the ranking of establishments with respect to wage rates.

When we examine the relationship of establishment characteristics to the representation of women and to the wage standing of the firm, we find in general that firm characteristics that are positively related to wage rates are negatively related to the representation of women and vice versa. The fact that industry is found to be an important explanatory variable in both cases suggests that industry segregation does exist, and that it is related to the wage standing of firms in the industry.

4

Occupational Wage Rates and Employment Patterns

In this chapter we have selected a subsample of occupation-skill classes to test the hypotheses generated by our model with respect to wage rates and employment patterns when occupations are considered separately. It is postulated that, within the firm, base occupational pay rates are established for each job category and that individual pay differences among workers within occupational categories reflect only differences in seniority and merit (ability). Further, we posit the existence of a hierarchy of firms with respect to wage rates that determines the base pay rate that the firm may offer in each occupational category.

Within this model, discrimination is manifested primarily through employer hiring practices that deny women access to the higher-wage establishments. These practices are seen to result in, on the one hand, sex segregation by establishment within occupational categories and, on the other hand, pay differentials by sex within occupational categories that are primarily related to differences in wage rates among firms rather than to differences in wage rates within firms.

The features of this model may be contrasted to the operation of an unprejudiced system, under the same set of assumptions. In such a system, sex would not be a barrier to entry into the firm. Thus the sex composition of the establishment's occupational work force would be consistent with a selection process in which the sex of the worker hired was solely the result of random processes. Intrafirm pay differentials by sex within occupational categories would reflect differences in seniority and merit, while the advantage of employment in high-wage firms, and the burden of employment in low-wage firms, would be equally shared between men and women. Thus the sex differential in wages would be expected to be relatively small, and to be primarily the result of intrafirm pay differences.

At the most basic level, the impact of discrimination may be discerned by comparing the actual distribution of men and women among establishments and the wage outcomes of workers by sex with the situation that would obtain in an unprejudiced system. However, some caution must be exercised in this regard, particularly in interpreting the wage data presented in this chapter. While it would be tempting to attribute all of the sex differentials in wage rates associated with interfirm pay differences to the exclusionary behavior of high-wage firms, in the absence of direct data on the personal characteristics of individual workers such an approach cannot be justified. On the one hand, it is

45

possible that the average quality of male labor is higher than the average quality of female labor and that such quality differences explain some portion of the sex differential. If this were the case, the impact of exclusion on pay differences would be overestimated. On the other hand, it is equally possible that, in the presence of sex discrimination in upgrading and promotion, as well as of other barriers to occupational mobility, female labor may be of higher average quality than male labor within specific occupational categories. In this case, the impact of exclusion on pay differences would be underestimated.

Both possibilities find empirical support in a study by Mary Hamilton (1973, p. 45) of intraoccupational sex differences in wages. After controlling for individual differences in worker quality associated with such variables as age, education, experience, training and seniority, she found that the unexplained sex differential was 11 percent of the male wage (65 percent of the gross sex differential) among accountants and 14 percent of the male wage (156 percent of the gross sex differential) among tabulating machine operators. Hamilton's study is particularly noteworthy in its controls for labor market experience. This factor has been argued by Mincer and Polachek (1974) to be an important contributor to the sex differential in earnings.

Moreover, it may be argued that, even in the presence of additional data, the impact on wage differences of discrimination through exclusion would be difficult to measure. Labor turnover, and thus the average level of seniority of workers within the establishment, is not a function solely of the personal characteristics of workers. The wage and promotion policies of the firm must also be considered. Further, were direct measures of labor productivity obtainable, these would not take into account the effect of the wage and personnel practices of the firm on the diligence and effort of the establishment work force, nor interfirm differences in the effectiveness of on-the-job training programs or opportunities.[1]

While we argue on the basis of theoretical considerations as well as empirical evidence that it is unlikely that interfirm pay differences are due solely to interfirm differences in the productivity-related characteristics of workers, in the absence of additional data it is not possible in specific cases to distinguish the intraoccupational differential resulting from individual characteristics from that resulting from other variables. Thus we trace the broad pattern of the relationship between differences in the distribution of men and women among firms and the male-female pay differential within occupational categories.

The occupation-skill classes included in the study of occupational wage rates and employment patterns are shown in Table 4-1. We shall refer to each occupation-skill grade as an occupational category. Empirical results have been reported for cities in which at least fifty firms contained observations on the occupational category, and in which at least seventy workers of each sex were employed in the sampled firms. Since occupational categories are considered separately, the designation of a firm as *segregated* or *integrated* is occupation

Table 4-1
Job Categories Included in the Study of Occupational Employment Patterns and Wage Rates

---

Office occupations
  Accounting clerk
    Class A
    Class B
  Order clerk
  Payroll clerk
  Office boy/girl
  Tabulating machine operator
    Class A
    Class B

Professional and technical occupations
  Systems analyst
    Class B
  Computer programer
    Class A
    Class B
    Class C
  Computer operator
    Class B

---

specific, referring only to the sex composition of employment within the occupational category.

A model is developed to test for the existence of sex segregation by firm within occupational categories, and findings on the magnitude of this type of employment segregation are reported for the sample of occupations and cities. The average wages of male and female workers are then examined by sector of employment, where sector is determined by whether the establishment employs all men, all women, or both men and women within the occupational category. A method is then derived to estimate the contribution of pay differences among firms and pay differences within firms to the occupational pay differential by sex. Our findings with respect to the magnitude of these two sources of the pay differential are reported.

Sex-Segregation by Establishment: Measurement and Magnitude

The model predicts that within occupational categories men and women will not be randomly distributed among firms, but rather that intraoccupational segregation will be present. The criterion for the existence of intraoccupational segregation is whether, for given occupational categories, each sex tends to work together within the same establishment to a significantly greater extent than would occur by chance. Thus if one were to view the distribution of establishments according to the proportion that women comprise of each firm's occupational work force, this criterion would be met if there were a higher concentration of establishments in the tails of the distribution, employing relatively high or low proportions of women, than would be expected if the laws of chance were observed. The first requirement for applying this criterion is to specify the distribution of establishments that would obtain if the sex of the employee hired were the result of a random process.

A Model of Random Hiring

We here develop a model which enables us to specify the distribution of firms with respect to the sex composition of occupational employment under conditions of random hiring. We may then compare this theoretical distribution of establishments to the actual distribution to determine for each occupational category whether sex segregation by firm within occupations exists.

For each occupation and city, let:

p = the proportion of the pool of individuals with the requisite occupational skills that is female.

$q = 1 - p$ = the proportion of the labor pool that is male.

x_i = the number of women employed in the occupation in firm i.

n_i = the total number of employees in the occupation in firm i.

$p_i = x_i/n_i \times 100$ = the percentage that women comprise of all workers in the occupation in firm i.

Then, x_i may be viewed as the outcome of n_i trials of an experiment where each trial consists of selecting an individual at random from the labor pool where the probability of obtaining a woman is p and the probability of obtaining a man is q. The binomial probability distribution may be employed to obtain the probability that x_i takes on any specified value (to be completely accurate we would have to postulate that the firms sample from the labor pool not only at random, but with replacement since it is only in this case that the outcomes of the n_i experiments can be independent):

$$f_i(x = x_i) = \binom{n_i}{x_i} p^{x_i} q^{(n_i - x_i)} \qquad (4.1)$$

To apply the model, establishments were grouped according to the number of employees in the occupational labor force. Each size category was composed of firms with the same value of n_i. The possible outcomes, x_i, were grouped into twelve categories according to the value of p_i. The twelve sex composition categories are: $p_i = 0$, $0 < p_i < 10$, $10 \leqslant p_i < 20$, $20 \leqslant p_i < 30$, ... $90 \leqslant p_i < 100$, $p_i = 100$.

Let:

n_j = the number of firms in the jth size category.

p_{jk} = the probability that a firm selected at random from the jth size class has a value of p_i that falls in the kth sex composition category.

e_{jk} = the expected number of firms in the jth size class and the kth sex composition category.

E_k = the total expected number of firms in the kth sex composition category.

P_k = the probability of obtaining a firm in the kth sex composition category, given the size distribution of firms.

Then, p_{jk} may be computed from (4.1) as:

$$p_{jk} = f(x_a \leqslant x \leqslant x_b) = \sum_{i=a}^{b} f_i(x = x_i) \tag{4.2}$$

Using the standard formula for expected value, e_{jk} may be computed as:

$$e_{jk} = p_{jk} \cdot n_j \tag{4.3}$$

The e_{jk} represent the theoretical distribution of firms by the sex composition of establishment employment disaggregated by size category. To find the theoretical frequencies for the N firms in the sample, we may sum across size categories:

$$E_k = \sum_j e_{jk} \tag{4.4}$$

And the theoretical probabilities for the sample may be defined as:

$$P_k = E_k / N \tag{4.5}$$

Finally, the chi-square "goodness of fit" test may be employed to determine whether the theoretical probabilities are correct or the disparity between the observed and the expected frequencies is large enough to reject the hypothesis of randomness.

If we wish to examine the distribution of male and female workers among establishments that would prevail under the conditions of random hiring, the worker distributions may be derived directly from the theoretical establishment distributions. Let:

n_{ij} = the number of employees in the occupational work force in firms included in the jth size class.

$\bar{p}_{ik}$ = the arithmetic mean of the p_i included in the kth sex composition category divided by 100.

f_{jk} and m_{jk} = the expected number of women and men respectively employed in establishments which fall into the jth size class and kth sex composition category.

F_k and M_k = the total expected number of women and men respectively employed in firms included in the kth sex composition category.

Then we may approximate f_{jk} and m_{jk} in the following way:

$$f_{jk} = e_{jk} \cdot n_{ij} \cdot \bar{p}_{ik} \qquad (4.6)$$

$$m_{jk} = (e_{jk} \cdot n_{ij}) - (f_{jk}) \qquad (4.7)$$

And F_k and M_k may be obtained by summation:

$$F_k = \sum_j f_{jk}$$

$$M_k = \sum_j m_{jk} \qquad (4.8)$$

While the worker distributions yield no new information in terms of possible hypothesis testing, they may be employed to compute the index of segregation, which in this case is a summary measure of the degree of intraoccupational segregation.

Conceptual Problems in the Application of the Model

Conceptually, the application of this model to establishment hiring poses certain problems of interdependence of outcomes. No difficulty would arise if firms sampled with replacement from the labor pool. However, since it is not reasonable to assume that firms do so, it may be helpful to consider whether problems of interdependence are serious enough to cast doubt on the ability of the theoretical distribution to serve as a fair and reasonable test for the existence of intraoccupational segregation.

The first area in which a question of interdependence arises is in the computation of p_{jk} in Equation (4.2). It may be recalled that we viewed the number of women employed in the establishment, x_i, as the outcome of n_i trials of an experiment where each trial consists of selecting an individual at random from the labor pool. If firms were to sample from the labor pool with replacement, p, the probability of selecting a woman would be constant from trial to trial, and the outcome of each trial could be viewed as independent. However, when the firm samples without replacement from the labor pool, p is not constant, but rather changes slightly from trial to trial as either a man or a woman is selected. This type of interdependence could be modeled with the hypergeometric distribution. However, the larger the total universe (in this case the total labor pool) relative to the sample size (in this case the size of the firm), the smaller the divergence between the results obtained with the hypergeometric distribution and those obtained with the binomial distribution. It is doubtful that even the largest firms are sufficiently large relative to the labor pool to warrant the use of the hypergeometric distribution. Moreover, the utilization of the hypergeometric distribution poses its own problems, the most serious being the necessity of specifying and estimating the size of the total universe or labor pool.

A question of interdependence also arises in the computation of e_{jk} in Equation (4.3). Such a computation gives us the expected outcome of n_j replications of the experiment in which n_i workers are selected at random from the labor pool when the constant probability of obtaining a woman is p. Clearly such a computation requires independence of outcome of the n_j experiments. However, in the real world there would be some interdependence of outcomes among all firms, inside and outside the sample, and within and among size categories. The nature of this interdependence is difficult to specify. Certainly the labor pool, comprised of available individuals with the requisite occupational skills, includes some presently employed workers as well as those presently unemployed. Indeed some workers in the labor pool may be presently employed in other occupations as well as by other firms. Thus we do not have a simple form of interdependence whereby a worker employed by one firm is completely unavailable to other firms, and vice versa. While it is easy enough to imagine scenarios in which interdependence among establishments would be significant, most would involve a substantial departure from random behavior on the part of at least some of the firms or substantial differentials in interfirm mobility between male and female workers. Thus it was felt that considerations of interdependence among firms did not seriously challenge the applicability of the model.

An additional conceptual problem arises when the temporal dimension of the hiring process is considered. The representation of women in the occupational labor force of the establishment is the outcome of a selection procedure that takes place over a considerable, although unknown, period of time. It is possible that p has varied over time and that some of the interfirm differential in female employment reflects the time period in which the bulk of the establishment's occupational work force was recruited. In this sense, our estimate of p, the proportion that women presently comprise of total occupational employment, may be considered to reflect the average representation of women in the labor pool over time rather than the actual availability of women each time the firm hires an additional worker. However, it is doubtful that this factor could account for a uniform pattern of intraoccupational segregation in a wide variety of occupational categories.

In most cases, the actual distribution of establishments by sex composition of occupational employment is so heavily concentrated at both tails of the distribution that only radical changes in the proportion that women comprise of new entrants to the occupational labor force could produce this result (see Appendix Table B-1). Moreover, in Chapter 4 we present evidence of the existence of establishment and industry segregation. Thus, for the temporal dimension of the hiring process to be the sole explanation for the observed patterns of sex segregation, it would be necessary for firms and industry groups to follow similar time patterns of recruitment across occupational categories, and for occupational categories to exhibit similar time patterns of changes in the level of p.

The Extent of Intraoccupational Segregation

To use the foregoing model to assess the magnitude of intraoccupational segregation, it is necessary to specify an estimate of p, the female proportion of the total labor supply pool in each occupation. We have here estimated p as the proportion women represent of all those actually employed in the occupation in each city. (P was estimated directly from our sample. Since the sample of establishments used by the Bureau of Labor Statistics in the *Area Wage Surveys* is a stratified and not a random sample, each observation was given its appropriate weight.) The size of the group of workers presently employed in an occupational category is a narrow definition of the pool of individuals with the requisite occupational skills. However, our definition of intraoccupational segregation takes as given the extent of interoccupational segregation, that is, the proportion that women comprise of total employment in each occupational category. Thus this estimate of p is consistent with our definition.

The way in which the theoretical distribution of establishments is generated from the size classes is illustrated in Table 4-2 for class A accounting clerks in Boston. The expected distributions shown in the table were derived from the

Table 4-2
Expected and Actual Distribution of Firms by Percent Female Employees and Size of Firm: Class A Accounting Clerks, Boston

Size of Firm	Distribution (numbers)	0	1-9	10-19	20-29	30-39	40-49	50-59	60-69	70-79	80-89	90-99	100	Total
1	Expected	11.63	0.0	0.0	0.0	0.0	0.0	0.0	0.0	0.0	0.0	0.0	26.37	38
	Actual	12.00	0.0	0.0	0.0	0.0	0.0	0.0	0.0	0.0	0.0	0.0	26.00	38
2	Expected	2.53	0.0	0.0	0.0	0.0	0.0	11.47	0.0	0.0	0.0	0.0	13.00	27
	Actual	5.00	0.0	0.0	0.0	0.0	0.0	4.00	0.0	0.0	0.0	0.0	18.00	27
3	Expected	0.52	0.0	0.0	0.0	3.51	0.0	0.0	7.96	0.0	0.0	0.0	6.02	18
	Actual	2.00	0.0	0.0	0.0	4.00	0.0	0.0	2.00	0.0	0.0	0.0	10.00	18
4	Expected	0.12	0.0	0.0	1.11	0.0	0.0	3.79	0.0	5.73	0.0	0.0	3.25	14
	Actual	3.00	0.0	0.0	1.00	0.0	0.0	0.0	0.0	0.0	0.0	0.0	10.00	14
5	Expected	0.02	0.0	0.0	0.21	0.0	0.97	0.0	2.19	0.0	2.49	0.0	1.13	7
	Actual	0.0	0.0	0.0	0.0	0.0	0.0	0.0	0.0	0.0	4.00	0.0	3.00	7
6-9	Expected	0.01	0.0	0.12	0.28	0.87	0.80	4.29	4.62	4.82	5.41	0.0	1.79	23
	Actual	1.00	0.0	0.0	1.00	2.00	0.0	3.00	4.00	4.00	0.0	0.0	8.00	23
10-19	Expected	0.0	0.0	0.0	0.02	0.16	0.61	2.04	4.17	4.14	2.18	0.58	0.10	14
	Actual	0.0	0.0	0.0	1.00	3.00	0.0	2.00	3.00	0.0	0.0	0.0	5.00	14
20-39	Expected	0.0	0.0	0.0	0.0	0.01	0.12	0.90	3.45	3.21	1.20	0.10	0.0	9
	Actual	0.0	0.0	0.0	0.0	0.0	1.00	1.00	0.0	0.0	1.00	2.00	4.00	9
40+	Expected	0.0	0.0	0.0	0.0	0.0	0.01	0.26	1.78	1.75	0.20	0.0	0.0	4
	Actual	0.0	1.00	0.0	0.0	1.00	0.0	0.0	0.0	0.0	0.0	2.00	0.0	4
Total	Expected	14.82	0.0	0.12	1.63	4.54	2.50	22.74	24.17	19.65	11.47	0.68	51.66	154.0
	Actual	23.00	1.00	0.0	3.00	10.00	1.00	10.00	9.00	4.00	5.00	4.00	84.00	154.0

(Percent Female spans columns 0 through 100.)

Source: Computed from unpublished Bureau of Labor Statistics data collected for the *Area Wage Surveys* between April and November 1970.

Note: Size of firm refers to the number of workers employed as Class A Accounting Clerks in each firm. If p_i is the percentage that women comprise of total occupational employment in firm i, then the 12 sex composition categories above are defined as: $p_i = 0$, $0 < p_i < 10$, $10 \leq p_i < 20$, $20 \leq p_i < 30, \ldots 90 \leq p_i < 100$, $p_i = 100$.

application of the model of random hiring. The actual distributions are of firms in the sample by sex composition category.

It may be noted that the total expected frequencies do not approximate a normal curve, but rather tend to cluster within a number of the sex composition categories. For a given value of p, the distribution of establishments among size classes is the most important factor in producing this clustering. Size of firm affects the theoretical distribution in two ways. First, when n_i is small, p_i can take on only a limited number of values, due to indivisibilities. Thus, for example, when n_i equals 2, there are only three possible values for p_i: 0, 50, and 100. Second, as n_i or the number of trials is increased, the expected distribution of establishments would tend to cluster more tightly around p. However, for smaller values of n_i, the expected distribution is more diffuse. This is a simple application of the Law of Large Numbers. In most cases, there are a relatively large number of firms with small values of n_i, and thus these firms heavily influence the total distribution.

The total expected and actual distributions of establishments by occupation and city are shown in Appendix B. Our findings are summarized in Table 4-3 which gives the chi-square values for two tests of the hypothesis of randomness in the distribution of firms by the sex composition of the establishment's occupational work force. The first test, X^2 (1), compares the actual to the expected frequencies of firms in three categories: firms employing only men, firms employing only women, and firms with mixed occupational work forces. The hypothesis of randomness is rejected in all cases. The second test, X^2 (2), compares the actual to the expected frequencies of firms in k sex composition categories, where the initial twelve categories were combined such that there was no category for which the expected frequency was less than 1. The hypothesis of randomness is again rejected in all cases.

The impact of the establishment distributions on male and female employment is shown in Table 4-4, which gives the actual and expected values of the index of segregation. The index employed here is similar in concept to Duncan and Duncan's Index used in Table 1-3. In this case the index has been defined so as to measure intraoccupational segregation. As stated earlier, it may take on any value between 0 and 100. In the present context, a value of 0 indicates that within the occupational category the distribution of women among the establishments in the sample closely approximates the distribution of male workers. Equivalently, this means that in each establishment the proportion of all those employed in the occupation who are women is roughly the same as the female share of total occupational employment. A value of 100 indicates complete segregation, with women employed entirely in firms that hire only female workers into the occupation, and men working in establishments that employ only male workers in the occupation.

The actual index of segregation is computed on the basis of the employment distributions of male and female workers in the sample. The expected index of

Table 4-3
Chi-Square Values

Occupation	P	N	$X^2 (1)$	$X^2 (2)$	k
Accounting clerk					
Class A					
Boston	0.694	154	43.51[a]	65.06[a]	9
New York	0.648	335	70.46[a]	118.53[a]	9
Philadelphia	0.731	171	28.06[a]	37.73[a]	7
Class B					
Boston	0.925	162	8.77[a]	13.44[b]	7
New York	0.759	322	66.01[a]	105.62[a]	7
Philadelphia	0.883	170	26.98[a]	36.89[a]	7
Order clerk					
Boston	0.615	67	55.07[a]	61.59[a]	9
New York	0.833	106	46.52[a]	53.84[a]	7
Philadelphia	0.712	62	35.55[a]	41.05[a]	7
Payroll clerk					
New York	0.855	223	23.60[a]	30.51[a]	7
Office boy/girl					
Boston	0.327	99	37.49[a]	49.43[a]	8
New York	0.248	279	113.51[a]	142.90[a]	8
Philadelphia	0.400	128	52.09[a]	66.09[a]	9
Tabulating-machine operator					
Class A					
New York	0.380	52	51.79[a]	55.50[a]	8
Tabulating-machine operator					
Class B					
New York	0.271	66	27.38[a]	33.51[a]	8
Systems analyst					
Class B					
New York	0.149	93	13.55[a]	18.38[a]	7
Computer programer					
Class A					
New York	0.208	122	12.72[a]	21.55[a]	8
Class B					
Boston	0.411	76	21.02[a]	32.69[a]	9
New York	0.261	138	13.97[a]	21.82[a]	8
Philadelphia	0.184	83	5.58[b]	11.82[b]	7
Class C					
New York	0.309	84	13.14[a]	18.82[a]	8

Table 4-3 (cont.)

Occupation	P	N	$X^2(1)$	$X^2(2)$	k
Computer operator					
Class B					
New York	0.101	165	33.31[a]	34.18[a]	7
Philadelphia	0.103	110	24.96[a]	26.27[a]	7

Note: To compute $X^2(1)$ the expected and actual frequencies were combined into three categories: $p_i = 0$, $0 < p_i < 100$, $p_i = 100$. To compute $X^2(2)$ the expected and actual frequencies were combined into k categories such that there was no category for which the expected frequency was less than 1.
[a]Significant at the 0.5% level.
[b]Significant at the 5% level.

segregation utilizes the theoretical distributions derived from the application of the model of random hiring. While a fairly large degree of segregation would be expected even on the basis of random hiring (due to the large representation of firms with a small value of n_i), the differences between the actual and expected values of the index (shown in the last column of Table 4-4) are generally of considerable magnitude. Thus a sizable proportion of women (or men) would have to be reallocated among firms for the actual distributions to approximate a situation of random hiring on the basis of sex.

It is interesting to note, however, that while the hypothesis of randomness has been rejected for all occupational categories, the values of the index of segregation indicate that in general the magnitude of segregation is smaller in the systems-analyst and computer-programer categories. Inspection of the actual and expected distribution of firms by sex composition of establishment employment indicates a unique pattern among these classifications. While the actual number of male-only firms exceeds the expected number, the actual number of female-only firms is in every case less than the expected number, and the vast majority of women in each category are employed in integrated firms. This result may indicate a reluctance on the part of employers to entrust these highly responsible and skilled jobs to solely female work forces. However, it appears that, for a group of employers, mixed work forces may be just as acceptable as male work forces.

The apparent acceptability of mixed work forces in the systems-analyst and computer-programer categories may be due, in part, to the rapid growth in demand for workers in these fields in recent years. The *U.S. Census of the Population* (1973, table 2) records a twentyfold increase in the number of workers employed as systems analysts and computer programers between 1960 and 1970. Since the computer jobs are relatively new, their wage standing in the firm is less influenced by historical and customary patterns. Thus it may be possible for most firms to set an occupational wage rate for these categories that

57

Table 4-4
Actual and Expected Indices of Segregation by City: Selected Occupations

Occupation	City	Index of Segregation		
		Actual	Expected	Difference
Office				
Accounting clerk				
Class A	Boston	72.62	28.92	43.70
	New York	59.54	27.77	31.77
	Philadelphia	72.58	32.32	40.26
Class B	Boston	59.53	43.91	15.62
	New York	58.69	28.06	30.63
	Philadelphia	82.22	34.60	47.62
Order clerk	Boston	85.47	35.85	49.62
	New York	84.21	35.25	48.95
	Philadelphia	90.05	28.68	61.37
Payroll clerk	New York	82.66	56.65	26.01
Office boy/girl	Boston	74.65	31.31	43.34
	New York	·82.22	20.60	61.62
	Philadelphia	65.12	33.76	31.36
Tabulating-machine operator				
Class A	New York	84.65	26.45	58.19
Class B	New York	77.11	23.91	53.20
Professional and technical				
Systems analyst				
Class B	New York	40.83	27.30	13.52
Computer programer				
Class A	New York	53.12	34.91	18.21
Class B	Boston	51.78	31.13	20.65
	New York	43.85	33.97	9.88
	Philadelphia	65.85	42.82	23.03
Class C	New York	40.60	31.52	9.08
Computer operator				
Class B	New York	82.08	47.48	34.60
	Philadelphia	85.79	54.00	31.79

Source: Computed from unpublished Bureau of Labor Statistics data collected for the *Area Wage Surveys* between April and November 1970.

Notes: Within each city, the index of segregation is computed in the following way: Let p_{hi} equal the percentage that women comprise of the labor force in occupation h within establishment i. Establishments are grouped into 12 sex composition categories depending

Table 4-4 (cont.)

on the value of p_{hi}. The categories are: $p_{hi} = 0$, $0 < p_{hi} < 10$, $10 \leqslant p_{hi} < 20$, $20 \leqslant p_{hi} < 30$, ... $90 \leqslant p_{hi} < 100$, $p_{hi} = 100$. Let f_{hk} equal the percentage of all female workers and m_{hk} equal the percentage of all male workers in occupation h who are employed in firms included in the kth sex composition category. The index of segregation for occupation h is then:

$$S_h = \frac{\sum_{k=1}^{12} |f_{hk} - m_{hk}|}{2}$$

The actual index of segregation utilizes the employment distributions of male and female workers from the sample. The expected index of segregation employs the theoretical distributions.

is high enough to attract some male workers in the majority of cases. However, expanding demand, in combination with the necessity of recruiting workers with some training or skills in this area from sources external to the firm, may have induced employers to accept female workers more readily. (While some firms fill lower-level programer jobs through the promotion of experienced clerical workers, outside sources of supply are important. Some training is generally required of new workers, although on-the-job training is also important in the skill acquisition process (U.S. Department of Labor 1970-71), pp. 244-49).

While employment expansion was no less rapid among computer operators, this occupational category differs from the other computer jobs in the greater tendency of firms to rely on recruitment of its members from internal sources. Often when employers install electronic computers, they fill many of the operator positions by transferring presently employed workers from jobs as tabulating- and bookkeeping-machine operators, since such categories may no longer be needed after the computer is installed. In addition, both in the case of transferred workers and of those beginners hired from outside, the firm generally provides the training (U.S. Department of Labor 1970-71, pp. 278-79). Thus, wage rages in the computer operator category are expected to be more closely tied to rates of remuneration in clerical jobs than are the rates for programmers and systems analysts. The sex composition of the computer operator category within the firm is thus expected to more closely reflect the sex composition of the clerical occupations from which many operators are recruited.

The Relationship of Male and Female Wage Rates to the Distribution of Men and Women among Establishments

In assessing the importance of the pattern of sex segregation by establishment delineated in the preceding section, a crucial factor to be considered is the relationship between the differential distribution of male and female workers among establishments and the intraoccupational pay differential by sex. In this section, we attempt to shed light on this question by examining the pattern of pay rates by establishment. First, the pattern of male and female wage rates by sector of employment is considered. Second, a method to estimate the contribution of pay differences within firms and pay differences among firms to the aggregate pay differential by sex is derived, and our findings are presented.

Male and Female Wage Rates by Sector

Since segregated establishments are viewed in our model as representing the extremes of the wage distribution, it is expected that the average wage of women in segregated firms will be below that of women employed in integrated firms, while the average wage of men employed in segregated firms will be above that of men employed in integrated firms. This also implies that the pay differential by sex will be larger in the segregated sector than in the integrated sector. The case of unconstrained employer preferences does not predict the existence of wage differentials by sector. Employers determine whether or not to hire women by comparing the market-wide sex differential to their coefficient of discrimination.

The case of employee preferences does not necessarily predict the existence of wage differences by sector. However, if such differences do in fact exist, the opposite pattern from that of our model is expected. That is, since men must be paid a premium to induce them to work with women, the average wage of men employed in segregated firms will be less than that of men employed in integrated firms. Further, since a profit-maximizing employer with no tastes for discrimination would hire men only if this imposed no cost disadvantage, the higher wages of men in integrated firms might have to be subsidized by female employees. If female labor is available to all firms at a lower wage than male labor, it is not necessarily true that women will earn less in integrated than in segregated firms. However, if a sectoral differential does exist, this is the direction that would be predicted. This reasoning further implies that the pay differential by sex will be larger in the integrated than in the segregated sector.

It may be helpful to summarize these alternative predictions more concisely. Let:

W_{IF} = the average wage of women in integrated firms.

W_{SF} = the average wage of women in segregated firms.

W_{IM} = the average wage of men in integrated firms.

W_{SM} = the average wage of men in segregated firms.

Then, the three cases may be distinguished as follows:

1. Our model:

$$W_{IF} - W_{SF}/W_{IF} > 0$$

$$W_{IM} - W_{SM}/W_{IM} < 0$$

$$W_{IM} - W_{IF}/W_{IM} < W_{SM} - W_{SF}/W_{SM}$$

2. Unconstrained employer preferences:

$$W_{IF} - W_{SF}/W_{IF} \cong 0$$

$$W_{IM} - W_{SM}/W_{IM} \cong 0$$

$$W_{IM} - W_{IF}/W_{IM} \cong W_{SM} - W_{SF}/W_{SM}$$

3. Employee discrimination:

$$W_{IF} - W_{SF}/W_{IF} \leqslant 0$$

$$W_{IM} - W_{SM}/W_{IM} \geqslant 0$$

$$W_{IM} - W_{IF}/W_{IM} \geqslant W_{SM} - W_{SF}/W_{SM}$$

Before examining the empirical evidence with regard to these alternative hypotheses, it is important to consider how conclusive a test we are able to perform, given the limitations of the data. As noted earlier, it is our view that interfirm differences in pay rates generally exceed what would result from differences in the productivity-related characteristics of workers. It is not our contention that all interfirm wage differences unaccounted for by differences in the individual characteristics of workers actually represent cost differences per efficiency unit of labor, since establishment as well as individual characteristics influence labor productivity. Furthermore, costs of search and training must also be taken into account. While we hold this to be a reasonable view that is consistent with evidence from a variety of sources, it must be acknowledged that in the absence of additional data we cannot rule out the possibility that quality differences within the male work force or the female work force or both exist in sufficient magnitude to cause a reversal of some of the computed sectoral differentials. Thus our findings with regard to the merit of these alternative hypotheses must be considered as suggestive but not conclusive.

Mean wages by sector are shown in Table 4-5 for each occupational category and city. Let us first consider the clerical and computer-operator classifications, since our findings regarding the extent of segregation by firm are most uniform in these cases. In fifteen of the cases, the mean wage of women employed in integrated firms was above that of women employed in segregated firms, and in only three of these cases was the differential in favor of women employed in integrated firms less than 5 percent. In one case, that of messengers in New York, there was no difference. Among tabulating machine operators (class A) there was an 8 percent differential in favor of women employed in segregated firms; however, our estimate of W_{SF} was based on only twenty-four workers.

For male workers the results are somewhat uneven, but they do tend to support our model. The average wage rate of men employed in integrated firms was below that of men employed in segregated firms in twelve cases, although in six of these the differential in favor of men employed in segregated firms was less than 5 percent. Men employed in integrated firms had higher mean wages than men employed in segregated firms in five cases, although in only one of these was the differential greater than 5 percent.

Since there is only one case in which the pattern of differentials by sector goes against our hypothesis for both men and women, the one in which $W_{IF} - W_{SF}/W_{IF} < 0$ and $W_{IM} - W_{SM}/W_{IM} > 0$, the employee preference model does not appear to be confirmed. Similarly, the presence of differentials by sector is counter to the employer preference model.

A possible explanation for the few observed inconsistencies in the pattern of wage rates by sector is that, especially in the case of men, there is some overlap between the segregated and integrated sectors. That is, men are more highly represented in the higher-paying integrated establishments, while women are more highly represented in the lower-paying integrated establishments. This explanation will be confirmed if it is found in most cases, even within the integrated sector, that pay differences among firms explain a substantial proportion of the male-female pay differential.

The hypothesis that the male-female pay differential will be larger in the segregated than in the integrated sector is confirmed in the majority of cases. This finding follows directly from the fact that our hypotheses concerning intersectoral differences in male-female wage rates were supported in most cases.

With respect to systems analysts and programers, there are only three cases in which the absolute number of women employed in segregated firms is large enough to report, and even in these cases the number of observations is quite small. All three indicate that women receive higher wages in integrated firms. With respect to men, $W_{IM} - W_{IS}/W_{IM}$ is negative in three cases and positive in three cases, but the differential is small in absolute size in all six cases. This finding, in combination with the small size of the wage differential between men and women that is computed for all firms (in the case of class C computer programers there is a small differential in favor of women) seems to indicate that

Table 4-5

Average Wages of Men and Women by Sector of Employment: Selected Occupations

62

Occupation	Segregated Firms			Integrated Firms			All Firms			Pay Differential between S and I Firms[a] (Percentage)	Pay Differential between Men and Women[b] (Percentage)		
	W	N	s.d.	W	N	s.d.	W	N	s.d.		S Firms	I Firms	All Firms
A Accounting clerk													
Boston													
Men	$3.99	46	0.62	$3.63	299	0.40	$3.68	345	0.45	-10	21	7	11
Women	3.16	375	0.49	3.38	393	0.45	3.27	768	0.48	+7			
New York													
Men	4.16	190	0.53	3.88	671	0.60	3.94	861	0.60	-7	16	5	9
Women	3.49	525	0.53	3.67	801	0.45	3.60	1326	0.49	+5			
Philadelphia													
Men	3.83	126	0.50	3.78	133	0.51	3.80	259	0.51	-1	22	9	16
Women	2.97	414	0.47	3.43	339	0.57	3.18	753	0.56	+13			
B Accounting clerk													
Boston													
Men	3.45	10	0.79	2.94	109	0.37	2.98	119	0.44	-17	24	9	11
Women	2.64	576	0.31	2.67	753	0.34	2.66	1329	0.32	+1			
New York													
Men	3.38	98	0.41	3.23	505	0.46	3.26	603	0.46	-4	15	5	9
Women	2.86	894	0.42	3.06	1116	0.36	2.97	2010	0.40	+7			
Philadelphia													
Men	3.59	20	0.83	3.54	356	0.43	3.54	376	0.46	-2	32	23	28
Women	2.46	871	0.31	2.72	474	0.57	2.55	1345	0.44	+9			

Order clerk													
Boston													
Men	3.75	51	0.66	3.91	58	0.65	3.83	109	0.66	+4	32	20	30
Women	2.56	159	0.32	3.12	42	0.59	2.68	201	0.45	+18			
New York													
Men	3.85	24	0.64	3.77	119	0.47	3.78	143	0.50	−2	28	17	24
Women	2.77	433	0.37	3.11	157	0.40	2.86	590	0.41	+11			
Philadelphia													
Men	3.46	40	0.49	3.64	74	0.64	3.58	114	0.59	+5	31	23	33
Women	2.38	305	0.44	2.80	32	0.65	2.42	337	0.48	+15			
Payroll clerk													
New York													
Men	4.05	47	0.96	3.64	76	0.93	3.80	123	0.96	−11	17	5	11
Women	3.35	497	0.55	3.46	106	0.52	3.37	603	0.55	+3			
Office boy/girl													
Boston													
Men	2.39	202	0.24	2.37	144	0.18	2.38	346	0.21	−1	6	4	5
Women	2.24	65	0.23	2.27	188	0.15	2.27	253	0.18	+1			
New York													
Men	2.57	939	0.32	2.53	782	0.27	2.55	1721	0.30	−1	6	5	6
Women	2.41	356	0.20	2.40	905	0.16	2.40	1261	0.17	0			
Philadelphia													
Men	2.31	224	0.33	2.60	158	0.64	2.43	382	0.50	+11	9	9	5
Women	2.10	66	0.19	2.36	219	0.55	2.30	285	0.51	+11			

Table 4-5 (cont.)

Occupation	Segregated Firms			Integrated Firms			All Firms			Pay Differential between S and I Firms[a] (Percentage)	Pay Differential between Men and Women[b] (Percentage)		
	W	N	s.d.	W	N	s.d.	W	N	s.d.		S Firms	I Firms	All Firms
A Tabulating-machine operator													
New York													
Men	4.10	195	0.48	4.20	56	0.38	4.13	251	0.46	+2	1	10	7
Women	4.07	24	0.66	3.79	133	0.29	3.83	157	0.38	−8			
B Tabulating-machine operator													
New York													
Men	3.51	241	0.39	3.28	195	0.36	3.41	436	0.39	−7	25	0	13
Women	2.62	107	0.23	3.27	134	0.29	2.98	241	0.42	+20			
B Systems analyst													
New York													
Men	7.01	220	0.97	6.90	492	0.75	6.93	712	0.83	−2	c	5	6
Women	c	4	c	6.57	160	0.80	6.53	164	0.29	c			
A Computer programer													
New York													
Men	6.96	198	0.94	6.52	345	0.54	6.68	543	0.74	−7	c	2	4
Women	c	7	c	6.41	189	0.62	6.40	196	0.63	c			

B Computer programer

Boston

Men	4.86	110	0.58	4.91	210	0.55	4.89	320	0.56	+1	29	−1	2
Women	3.47	13	0.35	4.95	109	0.71	4.79	122	0.82	+30			

New York

Men	5.57	185	0.82	5.73	380	0.68	5.68	565	0.73	+3	11	1	1
Women	4.96	18	0.84	5.68	201	0.61	5.62	219	0.66	+13			

Philadelphia

Men	4.94	214	0.70	4.81	133	0.53	4.89	347	0.64	−3	c	−1	2
Women	c	7	c	4.83	87	0.53	4.79	94	0.56	c			

C Computer programer

New York

Men	4.55	109	0.61	4.89	228	0.47	4.78	337	0.54	+7	12	0	−1
Women	3.99	12	0.41	4.91	165	0.45	4.85	177	0.51	+19			

B Computer operator

New York

Men	3.94	677	0.61	4.12	271	0.50	3.99	948	0.58	+4	20	−2	14
Women	3.15	115	0.28	4.22	41	0.58	3.43	156	0.61	+25			

Philadelphia

Men	3.66	412	0.46	3.38	102	0.43	3.61	514	0.47	−8	21	2	17
Women	2.89	52	0.24	3.32	20	0.46	3.01	72	0.37	+13			

Source: Computed from unpublished Bureau of Labor Statistics data collected for the *Area Wage Surveys* between April and November 1970.

[a] Computed as $w_{IM} - w_{SM}/w_{IM}$ and $w_{IF} - w_{SF}/w_{IF}$ for men and women respectively.

[b] The pay differential for segregated, integrated, and all firms is computed as $w_{SM} - w_{SF}/w_{SM}$, $w_{IM} - w_{IF}/w_{IM}$, and $w_M - w_F/w_M$ respectively.

[c] Not reported because of small sample size.

the interfirm wage distribution is more compact in these categories. This result is consistent with our suggestion that employers are able to set the wage rates in these occupations at a level which is high enough in the majority of cases to attract some male workers.

A comparison of mean wages of male and female workers by sector of employment indicates for the most part that the distribution of men and women among firms is an important factor in pay differentials between male and female workers. However, this finding is only a first step in an examination of the relationship between the differential distribution of men and women among establishments and pay differentials by sex. While all of the wage differentials between men and women in the segregated sector may be associated with differences in wage rates among firms, the same relationship holds for some portion of the pay differential between men and women in the integrated sector. In the next section we examine the broader question of the contribution of pay differences within and among firms to the market-wide wage differential by sex.

The Contribution of Intrafirm and Interfirm Differences in Wage Rates to the Male-Female Pay Differential

Let us first consider the problem of estimating the contribution of intrafirm and interfirm pay differences to the sex differential for firms in the integrated sector. If there are k such firms, then for each occupational category and city, W_{IM}, the mean wage of male workers, and W_{IF}, the mean wage of female workers, may be computed as:

$$W_{IM} = \sum_{i=1}^{k} p_{im} w_{im} \qquad (4.9)$$

and

$$W_{IF} = \sum_{i=1}^{k} p_{if} w_{if} \qquad (4.10)$$

where

p_{im} = the proportion of all male workers in integrated firms employed in firm i.

p_{if} = the proportion of all female workers in integrated firms employed in firm i.

w_{im} = the mean wage of male workers employed in firm i.

w_{if} = the mean wage of female workers employed in firm i.

Two sources of variation between the male and female means may be identified. First is the difference between w_{im} and w_{if}, or the differential wage rate of men and women within each establishment. We label the absolute pay difference that is associated with pay differences within firms the *intrafirm effect*. Second is the difference between p_{im} and p_{if}, or the differential distribution of men and women among firms. This differential may be considered to be associated with pay differences among firms. We label the absolute pay difference which arises from this source the *interfirm effect*.

The task of partitioning the total male-female differential in the integrated sector between these two sources of variation may be conceptualized in the following way:

$$W_{IM} - W_{IF} = \sum_{i=1}^{k} p_{io}(w_{im} - w_{if}) + \sum_{i=1}^{k} w_{io}(p_{im} - p_{if}) \qquad (4.11)$$

where p_{io} and w_{io} represent the as yet unspecified weights.

The *intrafirm effect* would then be equal to:

$$INTRA = \sum_{i=1}^{k} p_{io}(w_{im} - w_{if}) = \sum_{i=1}^{k} p_{io} w_{im} - \sum_{i=1}^{k} p_{io} w_{if} \qquad (4.12)$$

As indicated in (4.12), the intrafirm effect may be viewed in two ways: first, as a weighted average of the wage differences by sex within each firm, and second, as the differential that would exist if men and women had an identical distribution among firms so that the only source of variation between the male and female means would be differential pay within firms.

The interfirm effect would be represented by:

$$INTER = \sum_{i=1}^{k} w_{io}(p_{im} - p_{if}) = \sum_{i=1}^{k} p_{im} w_{io} - \sum_{i=1}^{k} p_{if} w_{io} \qquad (4.13)$$

The interfirm effect may similarly be regarded in two ways: first, as a weighted average of the differential distributions of men and women among firms, and second, as the wage difference that would exist if within each establishment men and women received identical wage rates so that the only source of variation between the male and female means would be the differential distribution among firms.

It may readily be seen that this formulation raises the familiar index-number problems of arbitrariness and consistency, which we shall examine individually as they arise in this particular exercise.

The problem of arbitrariness may be stated quite simply. There are a wide variety of possible weights that might be employed, each of which would yield a different estimate of the relative magnitude of the intrafirm and interfirm effects. Moreover, there is little theoretical justification for preferring one set of weights over another. The two most obvious alternatives would be to utilize either p_{im} and w_{im} (the male distribution and the male wage) or p_{if} and w_{if} (the female distribution and the female wage) as the constant weights. A possible compromise would be to compute the intrafirm and interfirm effects in both ways. However, a serious problem of consistency would still remain.

The consistency problem arises because if both the intrafirm and interfirm effects are computed using a consistent set of weights, they will not necessarily sum to the total differential. To completely partition the total differential would require the utilization of an inconsistent weighting scheme. Thus it may easily be shown that:

$$W_{IM} - W_{IF} = \sum_{i=1}^{k} p_{im} (w_{im} - w_{if}) + \sum_{i=1}^{k} w_{if} (p_{im} - p_{if}) \qquad (4.14)$$

or

$$W_{IM} - W_{IF} = \sum_{i=1}^{k} p_{if} (w_{im} - w_{if}) + \sum_{i=1}^{k} w_{im} (p_{im} - p_{if}) \qquad (4.15)$$

However, the consistency problem may be solved if we employ a simple average of the male and female weights (this approach is recommended and further justified by Kitagawa 1955, pp. 1168-93):

$$p_{io} = \frac{p_{im} + p_{if}}{2} \qquad (4.16)$$

$$w_{io} = \frac{w_{im} + w_{if}}{2} \qquad (4.17)$$

When (4.16) and (4.17) are employed as weights, the estimated intrafirm and interfirm effects will sum to the total differential. Further, it may be shown that when the two effects are computed in this way:

$$INTRA = \frac{INTRA(M) + INTRA(F)}{2} \qquad (4.18)$$

$$INTER = \frac{INTER(M) + INTER(F)}{2} \qquad (4.19)$$

where (M) and (F) indicate that male and female weights have been used respectively.

Since there are no sound theoretical reasons for preferring any particular structure of weights, it was felt that this scheme was in some sense optimal since it provides for a solution of the consistency problem. Moreover, as can be seen in (4.18) and (4.19), these weights may be viewed as a compromise or summary measure since the results are equivalent to a simple average of the estimates derived from the utilization of male and female weights respectively.

In applying this method of analysis to the firms in our sample, one further problem must be considered. Many of the establishments employ entirely male or entirely female work forces within occupational categories. The total pay differential may be partitioned into two components by incorporating the results obtained for integrated firms using the appropriate weights.

If there are k firms which employ both men and women, m firms which employ only men, and n firms which employ only women, the intrafirm and interfirm effects may be computed as:

$$INTRA = \sum_{k=1}^{k} p_{io} (w_{im} - w_{if}) \tag{4.20}$$

and

$$INTER = \sum_{i=1}^{k} p_{im} w_{io} + \sum_{i=k+1}^{m} p_{im} w_{im} - \sum_{i=1}^{k} p_{if} w_{io} - \sum_{i=k+1}^{n} p_{if} w_{if}$$

$$= \sum_{i=k+1}^{m} p_{im} w_{im} - \sum_{i=k+1}^{n} p_{if} w_{if} + \sum_{i=1}^{k} w_{io} (p_{im} - p_{if}) \tag{4.21}$$

where p_{im} and p_{if} now represent the proportion of all male and female workers respectively employed in firm i, and p_{io} is computed as a simple average of p_{im} and p_{if}.

As can be seen in (4.20), the contribution of pay differences within firms to the total wage difference depends both on the size of such intrafirm wage differences and on the relative weight of the firm in total employment. The interfirm effect in (4.21) is computed by calculating male and female mean wages, substituting w_{io} for w_{im} and w_{if} in the case of integrated firms.

The results of the application of this estimation technique are shown in Table 4-6. The absolute wage differentials have been divided by the mean male wage to facilitate comparisons across cities and occupations. It may be recalled that our model predicts that intrafirm differences in wage rates between men and women will be relatively small compared to market-wide occupational wage differences. The intrafirm effect in integrated firms is a weighted average of mean wage differences between men and women within firms. Thus it is predicted that the magnitude of the intrafirm effect given in the first column of Table 4-6 will be small relative to the average pay differential between all male and female workers employed in the occupational category, given in column 6. Further, our model predicts that differences in wage rates among firms will

Table 4-6
The Contribution of Intrafirm and Interfirm Pay Differences to the Male-Female Pay Differential by City: Selected Occupations

Occupation	Integrated Firms (Male-Female Pay Difference as a Percentage of the Male Wage)			All Firms			Interfirm Pay Difference (As a Percentage of the Total)	
	Intrafirm	Interfirm	Total	Intrafirm	Interfirm	Total	Integrated Firms	All Firms
A Accounting clerk								
Boston	2.1	4.6	6.7	1.5	9.4	10.9	69	86
New York	0.8	4.6	5.4	0.5	8.2	8.7	85	94
Philadelphia	3.9	5.4	9.3	1.8	14.6	16.4	58	89
B Accounting clerk								
Boston	3.8	5.3	9.1	2.8	8.1	10.9	58	74
New York	0.1	5.2	5.3	0.1	8.6	8.7	97	98
Philadelphia	7.0	16.2	23.2	4.6	23.4	28.0	70	83
Order clerk								
Boston	8.1	12.0	20.1	2.8	27.3	30.1	60	91
New York	2.5	14.9	17.4	1.7	22.6	24.3	85	93
Philadelphia	11.6	11.6	23.2	3.1	29.4	32.5	50	90
Payroll clerk								
New York	0.4	4.8	5.2	0.4	10.9	11.3	91	96
Office boy/girl								
Boston	2.7	1.3	4.0	1.6	3.3	4.9	31	67
New York	-2.2	7.4	5.2	-1.2	7.1	5.9	a	a
Philadelphia	1.9	7.2	9.1	1.4	3.9	5.3	79	74

A Tabulating-machine operator							
New York	-3.3	9.9	-2.6	9.8	7.2	a	a
B Tabulating-machine operator							
New York	-4.7	0.4	-2.5	15.0	12.5	a	a
B Systems analyst							
New York	3.5	4.8	2.9	2.9	5.8	26	50
A Computer programer							
New York	0.1	1.8	0.0	4.3	4.3	92	99
B Computer programer							
Boston	-0.6	-0.7	-0.5	2.6	2.1	14*	a
New York	1.2	1.0	0.9	0.1	1.0	b	10
Philadelphia	-0.4	-0.5	-0.1	2.2	2.1	20*	a
C Computer programer							
New York	—	0.0	0.1	-1.5	-1.4	—	a*
B Computer operator							
New York	0.4	-2.4	0.0	14.1	14.1	a*	100
Philadelphia	1.2	1.9	0.3	16.3	16.6	37	98

Source: Computed from unpublished Bureau of Labor Statistics data collected for the *Area Wage Surveys* between April and November, 1970.
[a] The percentage of the total pay difference that is due to interfirm differences in pay rates is greater than 100.
[b] The percentage of the total pay difference that is due to interfirm differences in pay rates is less than zero.
*The female pay rate exceeds the male pay rate.

account for a high proportion of the male-female differential in all firms, and for a substantial proportion of the differential between men and women employed in integrated firms. The proportion of the male-female wage differential in all firms that is accounted for by differences in wage rates among firms is shown in column 8, while interfirm wage differences as a percent of the male-female wage differential in integrated firms is given in column 7.

The employee discrimination model predicts exactly the opposite of these results if differentials by sector exist. That is, wage differentials should be largest when men and women are employed together in the same firm, and intrafirm differences in wage rates will account for a high proportion of the total pay differential.

The results presented in Table 4-6 support our hypotheses. In most cases the intrafirm effect in integrated firms is absolutely quite small. The average intrafirm pay differential is greater than 5 percent in only three cases: Class B accounting clerks in Philadelphia, and order clerks in Boston and Philadelphia. Moreover, in each of those three cases the magnitude of the intrafirm pay difference is small relative to the average male-female wage differential in both the integrated sector and all firms. There are five cases in which average intrafirm pay differences are in favor of women.

Differences in wage rates among firms, the interfirm effect, account for a substantial proportion of the male-female pay difference in integrated firms. In fifteen of the nineteen cases in which the male wage rate is greater than the female wage rate, interfirm differences in pay rates account for 50 percent or more of the total differential. In two of the three cases in which female mean wage exceeds the male mean, interfirm differences in pay rates account for 20 percent or less of the total differential, indicating that the wage advantage of women is primarily the result of the favorable intrafirm effect.

The importance of interfirm pay differences is even more strongly demonstrated when we consider all firms. Of the twenty-two cases in which the male mean wage exceeds the female mean, the proportion of the differential which is accounted for by interfirm differences in wage rates is over 80 percent in sixteen cases and at least 50 percent in twenty-one cases.

The model works fairly well even when the systems-analyst and computer-programer categories are considered separately. The average magnitude of intrafirm differences in wage rates is less than 5 percent in all cases. Moreover, in four of the five cases in which the mean earnings of men in all firms exceed the mean earnings of women, interfirm wage differences account for 50 percent or more of the total differential. This suggests that the smaller average wage differences by sex among systems analysts and programers reflect more compressed interfirm wage differences in these occupations, but a distributional pattern by sex within this narrower band that is similar to the other occupations in the sample.

Again, it is important to point out that, in the absence of direct information on the productivity-related characteristics of workers, it is not possible to argue that the interfirm effect is entirely due to the exclusion of women from the higher-wage establishments. However, the consistency of the observed relationships strongly suggests that the differential distribution of men and women among establishments is of great significance in explaining the sex differential within occupational categories.

Conclusion

In this chapter we have tested the hypotheses generated by our model with respect to wage rates and employment patterns when occupations are considered separately. We have confirmed the existence of intraoccupational segregation by comparing the actual distribution of establishments by sex composition of occupational employment with the distribution that would obtain under the condition of random hiring. It has also been established that, for the most part, the average wages of male workers are higher in segregated firms than in integrated firms, while the average wages of women are, in general, higher in integrated establishments than in segregated establishments. Further evidence of the relationship between the differential distribution of men and women among establishments to the male-female pay differential within occupational categories is provided by the finding that intraoccupational pay differentials by sex are primarily the result of differences in wage-rates among firms rather than within firms.

5

Establishment Wage Rates and the Sex Composition of Employment

In the preceding chapter we have tested our model in terms of its implications for the employment distribution and wage rates of men and women when occupational categories are considered separately. It has been confirmed that, within occupational categories, male and female workers are differentially distributed among establishments to a degree in excess of what could be expected from the operation of random processes. Further, this differential distribution, which we have termed intraoccupational segregation, appears to be an important factor in the pay differential between male and female workers. In most cases, earnings differences between men and women in the same occupational category are primarily the result of differences in wage rates among firms rather than of differences in wage rates within firms. It may be recalled that within our model these differential employment patterns and wage outcomes for men and women were viewed as resulting from a predetermined wage hierarchy of firms. Within the context of this predetermined wage structure, employer hiring preferences were viewed as tending, in effect, to ration the higher-paying alternatives to male workers, while female workers would, for the most part, find employment in the lower-paying firms.

To verify the causal mechanism postulated in our model, it is necessary to consider occupations jointly to form a picture of establishment wage and employment patterns. Does there exist a hierarchy of firms with respect to wage rates? To answer this question in the affirmative, the relative wage standing of the firm with respect to one occupational category must be correlated with its ranking with respect to other categories. In addition, the wage standing of the firm must be estimated, holding the effect of the sex of the workers employed constant. That is, both male and female workers must receive higher wages than they would otherwise obtain when they are employed in the higher-paying establishments, while both sexes must earn less when employed by the lower-paying firms. Only if these two conditions are met can we confirm the existence of a wage hierarchy among establishments which may be viewed as a determinant of, rather than a response to, the sex of the job incumbents.

In the model, this wage hierarchy among firms is viewed as producing differential establishment patterns with respect to the employment of women, or what we have termed establishment segregation. For this to be the case, it is required that the standing of the firm with respect to the representation of women in one occupational category be positively correlated with its ranking with respect to other categories. Finally, our model implies that the ranking of

75

the firms with respect to wage rates will be inversely related to the ranking of firms with respect to the representation of women.

We are also concerned with the establishment characteristics that generate the postulated wage hierarchy of firms that we have to this point considered to be predetermined. The impact on the wage standing of the firm of its size, industry, and union status is examined. The relationship of these factors to the representation of women in the establishment is also explored. The expectation is that establishment characteristics that are associated with higher wages will also be associated with a lower representation of women, and vice versa. Further, our view as to the importance of product market competition in enforcing homogeneity within industry groupings implies that industry would be an important variable in the determination of both the wage rates and the employment of women.

Establishment Wage Rates and Employment Patterns

Regression analysis with binary explanatory variables has been employed to examine the question of establishment differences in wage and employment patterns. This approach produces results equivalent to those of analysis of variance, but has the advantage that an equal number of observations in each cell is not required. Moreover, the use of regression analysis enables us to estimate coefficients for each firm that summarize its standing within the local labor market with respect to the wages paid to its employees and with respect to the representation of women. These coefficients will then be used as the dependent variables in the analysis of the determinants of wage and employment patterns.

The following relation was estimated for each labor market to test for the existence of interfirm differences in wage rates across occupational categories and sex groups (since our estimate of w_i is based on grouped data with unequal observations in each cell, observations have been weighted by the square root of employment to correct for the heteroskedasticity introduced by such grouping):

$$w_i = \alpha + \gamma S_i + \beta_1 O_{i1} + \ldots + \beta_m O_{im} + \delta_1 F_{i1} + \ldots + \delta_n F_{in} + \epsilon_i \quad (5.1)$$

where:

w_i = the mean wage of workers in the hth sex category, jth occupation group and kth firm.

S_i = 1 if the observation is on male workers and 0 otherwise.

O_{ij} = 1 if the observation is on the jth occupational category and 0 otherwise. There are $m + 1$ occupational categories and m occupation dummy variables.

$F_{ik} = 1$ if the observation is on the kth firm and 0 otherwise. There are $n + 1$ firms and n establishment dummy variables.

The coefficients on the establishment dummy variables in Equation (5.1) are estimates of the dollar-per-hour difference between the mean wage of workers employed in firm k and in an arbitrarily omitted firm, holding constant the estimated effect of occupation and sex of workers on wage rates. To obtain more efficient estimates of the establishment coefficients, the entire sample of occupations was included in this and the succeeding analysis of interfirm differences in the representation of women. The hypothesis that there are no significant differences among firms with regard to mean wages may be formulated in terms of Equation (5.1) as a test of the null hypothesis that δ_1, $\delta_2 \ldots \delta_n$ are jointly equal to zero. The following F statistic is formed to test this hypothesis:

$$\frac{(SSR_Q - SSR_K) / (Q - K)}{SSE_Q / (N - Q)}$$

where:

$Q = m + n + 2$

$K = m + 2$

$N =$ the total number of observations.

As stated earlier, this test produces equivalent results to analysis of variance (Kmenta 1971, pp. 370, 415-18).

The rejection of the null hypothesis would imply the existence of a wage hierarchy among firms as we have defined it. That is, the wage standing of the firm would be consistent across occupational categories and for workers of both sexes. Were this not the case, the wage variation within firms would exceed the wage variation among firms, and the null hypothesis would be accepted. The rejection of the null hypothesis of no significant variation among firms does not, however, imply that none of the coefficients on the firm dummy variables are equal to zero, or equal to each other. Nor would such a finding be necessary to our argument.

Holding sex constant in the estimate of the firm coefficients is extremely important for our investigation of the relationship between the wage standing of the firm and the sex composition of establishment employment. Our expectation is that, after adjusting for the occupational mix of the establishment, men will comprise a higher proportion of the work force in firms which pay higher wages to both men and women, while women will be more highly represented in firms which pay lower wages to both sexes. It is in this sense that the wage standing of the firm may be viewed as determining the sex composition of its work force. However, were sex not held constant, the relationship between the establishment wage standing and the representation of women in the firm would become a virtual tautology. That is, since on average women receive lower wages, firms that employ a higher proportion of women would necessarily be "low-wage" firms.

The question of the representation of women in the establishment is approached in a similar fashion. The following equation is estimated for each city (observations have again been weighted by the square root of employment to correct for the heteroskedasticity introduced by the use of grouped data) so that:

$$p_i = a + b_1 O_{i1} + \ldots + b_m O_{im} + d_1 F_{i1} + \ldots + d_n F_{in} + e_i \quad (5.2)$$

where:

p_i = the proportion of all workers employed in the kth firm and the jth occupational category who are female.

The coefficients of the firm dummy variables in Equation (5.2) are estimates of the percentage-point difference between the proportion of workers who are female in firm k and in an arbitrarily omitted firm, holding constant the estimated effect of occupational category on the representation of women in the firms. The occupational dummy variables are necessary because the availability of women to the firm differs by occupational category. The test for establishment segregation in Equation (5.2) may be formulated, as in Equation (5.1), as a test of the null hypothesis that d_1, $d_2 \ldots d_n$ are jointly equal to zero. The rejection of the null hypothesis of no significant difference among firms in the representation of women implies the existence of establishment segregation, that is, that not only are there significant differences among firms, but these differences are consistent across occupational categories.

Since there exist differences among occupational categories in the possible scope of interfirm variation in the representation of women, the estimated values of the coefficients d_k will differ depending on which occupations are included in the analysis. For example, more variation is feasible in an occupational category in which women comprise 50 percent of total employment than in the case of a classification in which women comprise 10 percent or 90 percent of all workers. The inclusion of the latter group of relatively sex-segregated occupations would tend to yield smaller estimated values of the d_k. However, since some variation by firm is possible for every occupational category that we have included, it did not seem appropriate to discard this information by restricting the analysis to a relatively small group of highly integrated occupations. An additional consideration was the advisability of including the same sample of occupations in both the wage and proportion-female analyses. The inclusion of occupational categories with relatively high or low percentages of women tends to make it more difficult to obtain significant differences among firms with respect to the representation of women, thus strengthening our confidence in such a finding should it be obtained. (Establishments which contained observations only on relatively sex-segregated occupations were excluded from the sample.)

The estimated coefficients on the firm dummy variables in Equations (5.1) and (5.2) yield a ranking of firms with respect to wage rates and the representation of women for each labor market. Our findings are summarized in Tables 5-1 and 5-2. The F ratios for the significance of the group of establishment dummy variables are given in the last row of each table. All are significant at the 1 percent level. Thus we reject the null hypothesis of no difference among firms with respect to wage rates and the sex composition of employment.

The values of the coefficients have been expressed as deviations from the mean in each labor market to facilitate comparisons across cities. The establishment distributions are quite similar for the three cities. While there is a tendency for the distribution of establishments with respect to the value of both δ and d to cluster about the mean value for the local labor market, the range of variation is considerable. For example, in the case of the estimated values of the firm coefficients in the wage equation, we found that 22 percent of the firms in Boston, 31 percent in New York, and 26 percent in Philadelphia paid mean wages that were more than forty cents per hour above or below the average for the sample, after we controlled for the occupational mix of the establishment and the sex of the workers employed (this represents a pay differential of 14 percent in Boston, 12 percent in New York, and 15 percent in Philadelphia). Similar differences are exhibited with respect to the representation of women in the establishment. For 21 percent of the firms in Boston, 26 percent in New York, and 22 percent in Philadelphia, the proportion of women employed by the establishment deviated from the average for the labor market by over ten percentage points, after controlling for the occupational mix of the firm.

The values of the F ratios indicate that the probability is extremely small that the observed interfirm differences would be obtained by chance were the establishment means indeed the same. However, perhaps a stronger indication that this is not a random phenomenon is provided by the relationship between the ranking of establishments with respect to the value of δ and their ranking with respect to the value of d. Our model predicts an inverse relationship between the two variables and this is in fact what was obtained. The spearman rank correlation coefficient between the two variables is $-.35$ for Boston, $-.27$ for New York, and $-.26$ for Philadelphia. All are significant at the .001 level. A nonparametric statistic was employed because it seemed to be the most suitable test of the model. An additional consideration was that the exact values of the

Table 5-1
Distribution of Firms by Wage Standing of Establishment and City
(Percentages)

Deviation from the Mean ($)		Boston		New York		Philadelphia	
		n	percentage[a]	n	percentage[a]	n	percentage[a]
Over 1.00		5	1.9	5	0.9	8	2.3
0.81-1.00		6	2.3	14	2.4	5	1.4
0.61-0.80		5	1.9	22	3.7	12	3.5
0.51-0.60		5	1.9	15	2.6	9	2.6
0.41-0.50	(+)	9	3.4	36	6.1	14	4.0
0.31-0.40		14	5.3	34	5.8	14	4.0
0.21-0.30		19	7.2	51	8.7	26	7.5
0.11-0.20		29	11.0	59	10.1	31	9.0
0.01-0.10		22	8.3	47	8.0	29	8.4
0		8	3.0	12	2.0	10	2.9
0.01-0.10		41	15.5	55	9.4	43	12.4
0.11-0.20		29	11.0	48	8.2	43	12.4
0.21-0.30		22	8.3	62	10.6	35	10.1
0.31-0.40	(−)	22	8.3	38	6.5	25	7.2
0.41-0.50		14	5.3	29	4.9	16	4.6
0.51-0.60		5	1.9	28	4.8	16	4.6
0.61-0.80		7	2.7	25	4.3	8	2.3
0.81-1.00		1	0.4	5	0.9	2	0.6
Over 1.00		1	0.4	2	0.3	0	0.0
Total		264	100.0	587	100.0	346	100.0
F ratio		9.27		6.76		10.46	

Source: Computed from unpublished Bureau of Labor Statistics data collected for the *Area Wage Surveys* between April and November 1970.
[a]Rows may not sum to column totals due to rounding.

firm coefficients, δ_k and d_k, are subject to error, since they are stochastic variables. For this reason, somewhat more confidence may be placed in the rankings than in exact values. However, the computed values of the simple correlation coefficients were also highly statistically significant and negative in sign. (The values obtained were −0.34 for Boston, −0.21 for New York and −0.24 for Philadelphia.)

In this section we have demonstrated the existence of a wage hierarchy among firms and of establishment segregation. We have also shown the expected inverse relationship between the ranking of the establishment with respect to the

Table 5-2

Distribution of Firms by Representation of Women in the Establishment and City

(Percentages)

Deviation from the Mean (Percentage)	Boston		New York		Philadelphia	
	n	percentage[a]	n	percentage[a]	n	percentage[a]
Over 40	1	0.4	1	0.2	0	0.0
31-40	0	0.0	4	0.7	2	0.6
21-30 (+)	1	0.4	18	3.1	3	0.9
11-20	25	9.5	67	11.4	38	11.0
6-10	70	26.5	70	11.9	64	18.5
1-5	60	22.7	112	19.1	79	22.8
0	32	12.1	76	12.9	35	10.1
1-5	28	10.6	111	18.9	68	19.7
6-10	20	7.6	63	10.7	23	6.6
11-20 (−)	10	3.8	46	7.8	17	4.9
21-30	9	3.4	7	1.2	8	2.3
31-40	2	0.8	6	1.0	1	0.3
Over 40	6	2.3	6	1.0	8	2.3
Total	264	100.0	587	100.0	346	100.0
F ratio	2.00		2.28		3.78	

Source: Computed from unpublished Bureau of Labor Statistics data collected for the *Area Wage Surveys* between April and November 1970.

[a]Rows may not sum to column totals due to rounding.

representation of women and its standing in the wage hierarchy. These results are counter to the predictions of the unconstrained employer preference model and the employee preference model. It may be recalled that in the case of employer preferences it is expected that the firms which hire a greater-than-expected proportion of men will be those firms that prefer men and will hire women only at a discount. In the case of employee preferences, men are expected to receive higher remuneration when they work with women. Thus in both cases male and female wage rates are not expected to follow the same pattern by establishment. Yet we have shown the establishment wage hierarchy to be consistent across sex groups. And moreover it is seen that men comprise a higher proportion of workers in those firms which pay higher wages to both sexes, while women are more highly represented in firms which pay lower wages to both sexes. As in our comparison of the predictions of these alternatives in Chapter 4, we must bear in mind that in the absence of further information on

worker quality our findings regarding these alternative explanations are suggestive but not conclusive.

The Determinants of Establishment Wage Rates
and Employment Patterns

In this section we examine the relationship of establishment wage rates and
employment patterns to a number of establishment characteristics. The model
postulates that the establishment variables determine the standing of the firm in
the wage hierarchy and thus the prices offered for labor in the various
occupational categories. The differing availability of male labor to the high- and
low-wage firms in conjunction with employer hiring preferences then determines
the sex composition of employment. Although this model postulates that at the
micro-level the causation runs from wage rates to sex composition of employment, we have chosen to consider both d, the standing of the firm with respect
to the representation of women, and δ, the standing of the firm with respect to
wage rates, as dependent variables that are determined by the same set of
establishment variables (note that the number of observations is now equal to
the number of firms, and thus the subscript i rather than k is associated with the
establishment).

The logic of the model is illustrated by the following equations:

$$d_i = f(\delta_i, \phi_i) \tag{5.3}$$

$$\delta_i = f(E_{i1}, \ldots E_{in}) \tag{5.4}$$

$$= > d_i = f(E_{i1}, \ldots E_{in}, \phi_i) \tag{5.5}$$

where:

ϕ_i = employer preferences regarding the employment of women in
firm i.

$E_{i1}, \ldots E_{in}$ = establishment characteristics that are related to wage rates.

A simultaneous equation system is postulated in Equations (5.3) and (5.4),
where the variable ϕ is not observable, but will affect the relationship between d
and δ. Since this is a recursive system, it is possible to estimate (5.3) and (5.4)
directly. However it would also be correct to estimate the two structural
Equations (5.4) and (5.5). The latter course was adopted primarily for three
reasons.

First, the causal relationship between d and δ is not completely clear; that is, Equations (5.3) and (5.4) may be oversimplified. The maintenance of a low-wage position requires that the firm be able to attract an adequate supply of labor, or else some adjustment will be necessary. Since the low-wage firm relies on female labor to a greater extent than does the high-wage firm, the availability of female labor to the firm may have an impact on wage rates. It was thus deemed advisable to relate both d and δ to a set of establishment variables that are truly exogenous. Second, both d and δ are stochastic variables subject to measurement error. A stochastic dependent variable does not pose serious statistical problems. However there are difficulties in utilizing a stochastic independent variable (Kmenta 1971, ch. 9). The available solutions to the errors in variables problems are not particularly satisfactory, and thus the simpler approach of estimating the structural equations seemed preferable. (In particular the application of available solutions requires the assumption that the covariance of the error terms, that is the error in d and the error in δ, be zero. Considering the process by which d and δ were estimated, it seems quite likely that this condition would not be satisfied.) Third, it seemed possible that some of the establishment variables might be related to employer preferences, and thus have a direct effect on the proportion of women employed by the firm. While in general we would expect the coefficients of the establishment variables to be of opposite sign when δ and d are employed as dependent variables, it seemed worthwhile to test this expectation directly.

Empirical Results

To facilitate comparisons across cities, the coefficients of the firm dummy variables obtained through the estimation of Equations (5.1) and (5.2) were transformed into indices. To obtain the wage index, the estimated mean wage of the establishment (after controlling for occupation mix and sex composition) was divided by the average for all establishments in the labor market. Similarly, to obtain the proportion-female index, the estimated average proportion that women comprise of establishment employment (after controlling for occupation mix) was divided by the average for all firms in the labor market. Thus, for each city, if $\overline{w}_o$ = the estimated average wage in the omitted firm obtained from Equation (5.1), and $\overline{w}_i$ = the average wage in firm i, then $\overline{w}_i = \delta_i + \overline{w}_o$, and

$$WI_i = \frac{\overline{w}_i}{\sum\limits_{i=o}^{n} w_i/n}$$

Similarly, if $\overline{p}_o$ = the estimated average proportion of women in the omitted firm obtained from Equation (5.2), and $\overline{p}_i$ = the average proportion of women in firm i, then $\overline{p}_i = d_i + \overline{p}_o$, and

$$FI_i = \frac{\overline{p}_i}{\sum\limits_{i=o}^{n} p_i/n}$$

This standardization procedure involves only addition and division by a constant and therefore does not alter the rankings of firms, only the units in which the interfirm differences are measured.

The following regression equations were estimated to explain differences among establishments in wage rates and in the representation of women. (The dependent variables were obtained through the application of regression analysis, and, as noted earlier, are subject to measurement error. Estimates of the standard deviation of this error are available in the form of the estimated standard errors of the regression coefficients on the establishment dummy variables in Equations (5.1) and (5.2). Observations have been weighted by the inverse of the standard errors to correct for heteroskedasticity.):

$$WI_i = \alpha + \beta_1 I_{i1} + \dots + \beta_n I_{in} + \gamma_1 U_{i1} + \gamma_2 U_{i2} + \eta_1 S_{i1} + \epsilon_i \quad (5.6)$$

$$FI_i = a + b_1 I_{i1} + \dots + b_n I_{in} + g_1 U_{i1} + g_2 U_{i2} + h_1 S_{i1} + e_i \quad (5.7)$$

where:

I_{i0} = 1 if the firm is in the wholesale trade-durable goods industry (SIC 50) and 0 otherwise. This is the reference dummy for the industry variables.

I_{ij} = 1 if the firm is in the jth industry group and 0 otherwise.

U_{i0} = 1 if a majority of both plant and office workers in the firm are not unionized and 0 otherwise. This is the reference dummy for the union variables.

U_{i1} = 1 if a majority of both plant and office workers in the firm are unionized and 0 otherwise. (Three establishments in which a majority of office workers were unionized, but a majority of plant workers were not, were given a value of 1 for variable U_1.)

U_{i2} = 1 if a majority of plant workers in the firm are unionized, but a majority of office workers are not, and 0 otherwise.

S_{i0} = 1 if the firm employs between fifty and 999 workers and 0 otherwise. This is the reference dummy for the size of firm variable. (For the purposes of the *Area Wage Survey*, the Bureau of Labor Statistics includes in the sample only firms which employ fifty or more workers.)

S_{i1} = 1 if the firm employs 1,000 or more workers and 0 otherwise.

We refer to Equation (5.6) as the *wage regression*, and to Equation (5.7) as the *proportion-female regression*.

Before we discuss the regression results, some important qualifications are in order. First, the effect of industry on the wage standing of the firm and the representation of women in the establishment can best be tested when extremely fine industry classifications are employed. For our data, only two-digit SIC classifications are available. Further, it was necessary in some cases to form combinations of two-digit industries in order to obtain an adequate number of observations for each industry cell (see Appendix B-2). Thus our industry variable only approximates the product market distinctions that would provide the best test of the industry effect.

Second, while we are able to classify establishments by whether the majority of (plant or office) workers are unionized (covered by a collective bargaining contract), we have no further information on the characteristics of the union. Thus the union dummy variables provide only an imprecise indication of union power. Moreover, a common problem in the estimation of the impact of unions is that the effect of unionization on wage rates may be difficult to measure if nonunion firms pay union rates or higher ones to combat the threat of unionization (Lewis 1963). In addition, it is important to note that we are not able to assess the nonpecuniary benefits of unionization, which may be of considerable importance in workers' decisions to join unions (Ashenfelter and Johnson 1972, pp. 491-92).

Third, we have no information regarding the locus of wage control in the establishments in our sample. It has often been noted that in the case of multiplant firms, wage decisions may be made at national headquarters, leaving the local management little discretion to adapt to local labor market conditions. Such local establishments may tend to be either high- or low-wage firms in the labor market. Thus we expect that the omission of this variable will detract from the explanatory power of the model.[1]

Finally it is important to note that the sample of establishments is not well distributed by industry, union status, and size of firm. We have indirectly alluded to this problem by reporting the necessity of combining two-digit industries. However, when the data are cross-classified by more than one dimension, it is clear that we must be cautious in our interpretation of the regression results. See Appendix B-2 for the distribution of sample establishments by industry, union status, and size. For example, in each city there are a large number of two-digit industry classifications, and even major industry groups (e.g., finance, insurance, and real estate), that have no observations on unionized firms. Similar problems exist with the size variable. This means at minimum that we cannot be sure that the estimated union and size effects would be of the same magnitude in such categories as in the rest of the sample. More probably it suggests that it is not possible to estimate statistically the *pure* effect of industry, union status, or size of firm on the dependent variables. This is especially true since we have in cases combined two-digit industries into larger groupings. Of course, what we face here is not simply a statistical problem, but a reflection of economic reality. Interindustry differences in the distribution of establishments by union status and size of firm are an important factor in the explanation of wage differences among industries (Fuchs 1968, pp. 147-54). Moreover, there is considerable evidence of important interaction effects between industry characteristics and the impact of unions on wage rates (Segal 1964; Weiss 1966).

These problems are particularly serious in the case of Boston where considerable grouping of two-digit industries was necessary, and the absolute number both of unionized (plant and office) and of larger establishments (1,000 or more employees) was relatively small. Thus while the Boston regression results are included for the sake of consistency, it is not clear whether the data can support an analysis of this kind.

In light of these difficulties, the results presented in the section should be viewed primarily as a preliminary investigation of the importance of structural factors in the determination of the ranking of the firm in the local labor market with respect to wage rates and the representation of women in white-collar occupations. It is our view that the results are promising enough to warrant further exploration of this approach.

The regression results for the three cities are presented in Tables 5-3-5-5 (the sample size in each city has been slightly reduced by the deletion of firms with missing SIC codes). Two sets of regression results are reported for each city. The first set shows our findings for the estimation of Equations (5.6) and (5.7). The second set of regressions includes interaction effect(s) and must be regarded with particular caution due to the empty-cell and small-sample-size problem. Our findings with respect to the explanatory power of the regressions and the impact of the industry variables apply equally to both sets of regressions. We consider the differences between the two specifications in reference to the impact of union status and size of firm on the dependent variables.

All of the regression equations are statistically significant. The Boston proportion-female regressions are significant at the .05 level, while the remainder of the equations are significant at the .01 level, suggesting that the observed interfirm differences in wage rates and in the representation of women do, to some extent, follow discernible patterns with respect to economically meaningful establishment characteristics.

In each city we find that the proportion female regressions explain a considerably smaller proportion of the total variance in the dependent variable and contain fewer significant explanatory variables than do the wage regressions. This finding is susceptible to a number of interpretations. It may indicate the range of employer latitude in determining the sex composition of employment, suggesting that hiring preferences are important. However, it is also possible that, as noted earlier, the inclusion of relatively sex-segregated occupations in the estimation of Equation (5.2) tends to push the firm coefficients towards the mean, thus making it more difficult to obtain significant differences among firms or groups of firms.

The coefficients of the industry dummy variables in the regression equations indicate that there are significant differences among industry groups with respect to wage rates and the representation of women. Again, while this finding is weaker in the case of Boston, it is probably indicative of the aggregation problems. We have said that industry segregation occurs when workers in a sex group are employed together in the same industry to a greater extent than would be predicted by the laws of chance. The presence of significant coefficients for a number of the industry dummy variables suggests that such segregation does exist. In general, b_j, the regression coefficient for the jth industry category in the proportion female regression is of the opposite sign from β_j, the regression coefficient for the jth industry category in the wage regression. This result confirms our expectation that women are more highly represented in industries which pay lower wages to both men and women. (However, our results do not indicate a one-to-one correspondence between the wage standing of the industry and the representation of women, either in terms of a comparison of the absolute magnitude of the coefficients or in terms of their levels of significance in the two equations. Again, it is not clear whether this represents the effect of employer preferences or estimation problems in the dependent variable in the proportion female regressions.) While we have not explained the causes of the observed interindustry differentials, the existence of these differences suggests that product-market competition does enforce some degree of homogeneity in wage rates for office workers within industry groupings. This in turn suggests that wage differences do to some extent reflect differences in labor costs. In this regard, it appears likely that a finer industry classification would tend to produce sharper patterns.

The results for variable U_1 (plant and office workers unionized) were initially inconsistent across cities. For Boston a relatively large union effect was obtained in both the wage and proportion female regressions. In Philadelphia the union effect was more moderate, but significant, while in New York there was no statistically significant relationship. To test for the possibility that sectoral differences underlay these inconsistencies, a manufacturing-union variable was created to measure the impact of unions in this sector. (The manufacturing-union variable equals 1 if the firm is both unionized and in the manufacturing sector, and 0 otherwise. It should be noted that this variable measures the union effect only for those manufacturing industries which had observations on union establishments. This factor is of importance in the Boston regressions, where there is a serious empty cell problem.)

The results that are reported in the second set of regressions indicate that there is evidence of a significant union effect on the dependent variables in the manufacturing sector of all three cities. Among these firms, unionization of a majority of plant and office workers produced a positive effect on the wage index, and a negative effect on the proportion-female index. The large impact of manufacturing-union status on the dependent variables in the Boston regressions is based on only five observations on unionized manufacturing firms and thus its

Table 5-3
Wage and Proportion Female Regressions: Boston
(Absolute *t*-values)

Independent Variables	Regressions—without Interaction Effect		Regressions—with Interaction Effect	
	Wage I Coeff.	Fem I Coeff.	Wage I Coeff.	Fem I Coeff.
Industry				
Manufacturing				
Food and kindred products	−0.0456	−0.0175	−0.0682	−0.0068
	(0.97)	(0.30)	(1.50)	(0.12)
Machinery, except electrical	−0.0035	0.0015	−0.0076	0.0035
	(0.09)	(0.03)	(0.21)	(0.07)
Electrical machinery	−0.0709	0.0766	−0.0871	0.0843
	(2.00)	(1.76)	(2.54)	(1.93)
Other nondurable goods	−0.0442	0.0887	−0.0795	0.1016
	(1.36)	(2.13)	(2.47)	(2.47)
Other durable goods	0.0102	0.0565	0.0042	0.0535
	(0.26)	(1.04)	(0.11)	(1.10)
Transportation and public utilities	−0.0114	0.0338	0.0536	0.0030
	(0.26)	(.6195)	(1.19)	(0.05)
Retail trade				
General merchandise	−0.1489	0.1482	−0.1206	0.1348
	(3.85)	(3.12)	(3.19)	(2.80)
Other retail	−0.0545	0.0562	−0.0579	0.0578
	(1.46)	(1.22)	(1.61)	(1.26)
Finance and insurance				
Finance	0.0533	0.0066	0.0501	0.0080
	(1.56)	(0.16)	(1.53)	(0.19)
Insurance	−0.0328	0.0384	−0.0359	0.0398
	(1.08)	(1.03)	(1.23)	(1.07)
Services				
Personal services	−0.0895	−0.0277	−0.0973	−0.0240
	(1.69)	(0.42)	(1.90)	(0.37)
Business and repair services	−0.0020	0.0113	−0.0065	0.0135
	(0.06)	(0.29)	(0.21)	(0.34)
Miscellaneous services	0.0957	0.0007	0.0896	0.0035
	(2.36)	(0.01)	(2.29)	(0.07)
Union status				
Union	0.1437	−0.1338	0.0307	−0.0802
	(4.13)	(3.12)	(0.72)	(1.49)
Plant only	0.0127	−0.0312	0.0159	−0.0328
	(0.61)	(1.23)	(0.80)	(1.29)

Table 5-3 (cont.)

Independent Variables	Regressions—without Interaction Effect		Regressions—with Interaction Effect	
	Wage I Coeff.	Fem I Coeff.	Wage I Coeff.	Fem I Coeff.
Size of firm				
Size 1 (1,000 and over)	0.0337	−0.0012	0.0265	0.0022
	(1.95)	(0.06)	(1.58)	(0.10)
Interaction term				
Manufacturing and union			0.2791	−0.1323
			(4.37)	(1.66)
Constant term	0.9979	0.9982	1.004	0.9953
	(46.38)	(37.65)	(48.34)	(37.59)
Statistics				
Corrected R^2	0.15	0.05	0.22	0.06
F ratio	3.81	1.79	4.99	1.86
Observations	248	248	248	248

magnitude is questionable. The impact of unionization in the manufacturing sector in New York and Philadelphia is quite similar. Other things being equal, unionization increases the wage index by six percentage points in New York and eight percentage points in Philadelphia; similarly, it reduces the proportion-female index by six percentage points in New York, and seven percentage points in Philadelphia. These estimates are obtained by summing the coefficients on the union and manufacturing-union variables. The relative effect (in percentage terms) of unionization in manufacturing will differ by industry group and by size of firm. We have only indicated the constant absolute effect on the wage and proportion-female indices.

After removing the effect of these unionized manufacturing firms, there is no evidence of a positive effect on unionization on wage rates for the rest of the sample. (In Philadelphia, the estimated union effect in the first set of equations is dominated by the manufacturing firms which comprise 74 percent of unionized establishments, as contrasted to 28 percent in New York. In Boston, this appears to be due primarily to the large size of the union effect in the manufacturing firms, which comprise only 28 percent of union establishments.) This finding, tentative as it must be in light of the data problems, appears worthy of further investigation.

In contrast to our findings for the impact of organization among both plant and office workers, with one exception we find no statistically significant relationships between the dependent variables and the presence of a union

Table 5-4
Wage and Proportion Female Regressions: New York
(Absolute *t*-values)

Independent Variables	Regressions—without Interaction Effects		Regressions—with Interaction Effects	
	Wage I Coeff.	Fem I Coeff.	Wage I Coeff.	Fem I Coeff.
Industry				
Manufacturing				
Food and kindred products	−0.0309	0.0350	−0.0592	0.0706
	(1.29)	(1.08)	(2.37)	(2.09)
Apparel	−0.0997	0.0063	−0.1241	0.0382
	(2.27)	(0.11)	(2.83)	(0.64)
Printing and publishing	−0.0076	−0.0529	−0.0435	0.0041
	(0.35)	(1.74)	(1.87)	(0.13)
Chemicals	0.0061	0.0328	−0.0151	0.0580
	(0.26)	(1.02)	(0.61)	(1.74)
Machinery, except electrical	−0.0769	0.0128	−0.1109	0.0549
	(2.58)	(0.32)	(3.56)	(1.30)
Electrical machinery	−0.1239	0.0470	−0.1413	0.0685
	(5.28)	(1.48)	(5.94)	(2.12)
Instruments	−0.1198	0.0270	−0.1502	0.0645
	(4.16)	(0.69)	(5.02)	(1.59)
Miscellaneous mfg.	−0.1340	0.1093	−0.1476	0.1265
	(3.68)	(2.22)	(4.08)	(2.58)
Other nondurable goods	−0.0634	0.0523	−0.0813	0.0737
	(2.19)	(1.33)	(2.78)	(1.86)
Other durable goods	0.0141	−0.0194	−0.0011	−0.0011
	(0.65)	(0.66)	(0.05)	(0.04)
Transportation and public utilities				
Water transportation	0.0386	−0.1272	0.0510	−0.1424
	(1.20)	(2.92)	(1.59)	(3.27)
Air transportation	0.0097	0.0001	0.0214	−0.0144
	(0.40)	(0.00)	(0.87)	(0.44)
Communication	−0.0387	0.1035	−0.0181	0.0780
	(1.61)	(3.18)	(0.74)	(2.34)
Other transportation and public utilities	−0.0467	−0.0564	−0.0380	−0.0676
	(1.73)	(1.54)	(1.42)	(1.86)
Retail trade				
General merchandise	−0.1605	0.0872	−0.1435	0.0663
	(7.30)	(2.93)	(6.41)	(2.18)
Apparel and accessories	−0.0928	0.0266	−0.0835	0.0133
	(2.21)	(0.46)	(2.00)	(0.24)

Table 5-4 (cont.)

Independent Variables	Regressions—without Interaction Effects		Regressions—with Interaction Effects	
	Wage I Coeff.	Fem I Coeff.	Wage I Coeff.	Fem I Coeff.
Other retail	−0.0617 (1.83)	0.1049 (2.30)	−0.0567 (1.70)	0.0993 (2.19)
Finance, insurance and real estate				
Banking and credit	−0.0393 (1.92)	−0.0007 (0.03)	−0.0292 (1.41)	−0.0127 (0.45)
Brokers and investment offices	−0.0553 (2.65)	−0.0794 (2.81)	−0.0490 (2.36)	−0.0865 (3.07)
Insurance	−0.0532 (2.52)	0.0346 (1.21)	−0.0478 (2.26)	0.0284 (0.99)
Real estate	0.0413 (0.63)	0.0716 (0.80)	0.0298 (0.46)	0.0854 (0.97)
Services				
Personal services	−0.0822 (2.72)	0.0719 (1.76)	−0.0738 (2.47)	0.0610 (1.50)
Business and repair services	−0.0536 (2.69)	−0.0164 (0.61)	−0.0542 (2.55)	−0.0199 (0.74)
Other services	0.0230 (0.94)	−0.0450 (1.36)	0.0299 (1.23)	−0.0536 (1.63)
Union status				
Union	0.0098 (0.77)	0.0088 (0.51)	−0.0093 (0.65)	0.0353 (1.82)
Plant only	−0.0239 (2.09)˙	−0.0136 (0.88)	−0.0213 (1.87)	−0.0168 (1.09)
Size of firm				
Size 1 (1,000 and over)	0.0016 (0.18)	0.0058 (0.46)	0.0169 (1.47)	0.0161 (1.04)
Interaction terms				
Manufacturing and union			0.0715 (2.67)	−0.0997 (2.74)
Manufacturing and size 1			0.0462 (2.42)	−0.0537 (2.07)
Constant term	1.0583 (86.35)	0.9833 (59.25)	1.0625 (87.28)	0.9779 (59.26)
Statistics				
Corrected R^2	0.18	0.09	0.20	0.11
F ratio	5.60	3.14	5.82	3.43
Observations	572	572	572	572

Table 5-5
Wage and Proportion Female Regressions: Philadelphia
(Absolute *t*-values)

Independent Variables	Regressions-without Interaction Effects		Regressions with Interaction Effects	
	Wage I Coeff.	Fem I Coeff.	Wage I Coeff.	Fem I Coeff.
Industry				
Manufacturing				
Food and kindred products	−0.0377	0.0448	−0.0718	0.0611
	(1.02)	(0.95)	(1.97)	(1.28)
Apparel	−0.1026	0.1329	−0.1236	0.1527
	(1.95)	(1.98)	(2.40)	(2.26)
Printing and publishing	−0.0534	0.0071	−0.1013	0.0268
	(1.29)	(0.13)	(2.43)	(0.49)
Chemicals	0.0782	0.0312	0.0367	0.0508
	(2.42)	(0.75)	(1.12)	(1.19)
Primary metals	−0.0245	−0.1369	−0.0701	−0.1107
	(0.64)	(2.80)	(1.81)	(2.19)
Fabricated metals	−0.0864	−0.0248	−0.1200	−0.0090
	(2.18)	(0.49)	(3.04)	(0.17)
Machinery, except electrical	−0.1025	0.0005	−0.1443	0.0216
	(3.24)	(0.01)	(4.51)	(0.51)
Electrical machinery	−0.0867	0.0522	−0.1278	0.0792
	(2.59)	(1.32)	(4.01)	(1.90)
Other nondurable goods	−0.0208	0.0497	−0.0453	0.0629
	(0.57)	(1.06)	(1.26)	(1.33)
Other durable goods	−0.0074	0.0059	−0.0462	0.0278
	(0.26)	(0.16)	(1.60)	(0.73)
Transportation and public utilities	0.0238	0.0694	0.0342	0.0550
	(0.68)	(1.56)	(0.99)	(1.22)
Retail trade				
General merchandise	−0.1724	0.1662	−0.1011	0.1266
	(4.97)	(3.75)	(2.72)	(2.61)
Other retail	−0.0745	0.0182	−0.0287	0.0236
	(1.83)	(0.35)	(0.70)	(0.04)
Finance, insurance, and real estate				
Finance	−0.0674	0.0840	−0.0373	0.0724
	(2.15)	(2.09)	(1.19)	(1.77)
Insurance and real estate	−0.0444	0.0536	−0.0301	0.0482
	(1.57)	(1.48)	(1.08)	(1.33)
Services				
Personal services	−0.1372	0.0502	−0.1413	0.0483
	(2.82)	(0.81)	(2.99)	(0.78)

Table 5-5 (cont.)

Independent Variables	Regressions-without Interaction Effects		Regressions—with Interaction Effects	
	Wage I Coeff.	Fem I Coeff.	Wage I Coeff.	Fem I Coeff.
Business and repair services	−0.0679 (1.69)	−0.0000 (0.00)	0.0734 (1.88)	0.0026 (0.05)
Other services	−0.0442 (0.98)	−0.0419 (0.73)	0.0545 (1.24)	−0.0378 (0.65)
Union status				
Union	0.0768 (3.29)	−0.0453 (1.52)	0.0129 (0.32)	0.0390 (0.74)
Plant only	0.0108 (0.58)	0.0012 (0.05)	−0.0094 (0.51)	−0.0033 (0.14)
Size of firm				
Size 1 (1,000 and over)	0.0402 (2.70)	0.0187 (0.98)	−0.0333 (1.47)	0.0097 (0.33)
Interaction terms				
Manufacturing and union			0.0678 (1.69)	−0.1071 (1.78)
Manufacturing and size 1			0.1205 (4.10)	−0.0434 (1.13)
Constant term	1.0223 (47.40)	0.9856 (35.83)	1.0326 (48.99)	0.9815 (35.62)
Statistics				
Corrected R^2	0.21	0.10	0.26	0.11
F ratio	5.26	2.78	6.00	2.79
Observations	336	336	336	336

among a majority of plant workers. The exception, a small negative relationship between the wage index and blue-collar unionism in New York, may well be an artifact of the data. This finding regarding the impact (or rather the lack of impact) of blue-collar unions on white-collar wages is consistent with a number of other studies[2] and thus cannot easily be dismissed as due to pecularities in our sample (no success was obtained with interaction effects or other efforts to discern consistent relationships). Superficially, these findings appear to contradict two empirical observations. First is the evidence that blue-collar unionism is positively related to the wage rates of manual workers (Weiss 1966; Raimon and Stoikov 1969). Second is the observation that many firms tend to grant white-collar workers pay increases comparable to those negotiated with blue-collar unions, possibly to avert attempts at unionization (Kassalow 1967; p.

360). However, there may in fact be no contradiction, since it may be that white-collar wages are lower relative to blue-collar wages in establishments where the former group is unorganized than in nonunion firms or in firms where both groups are organized. This relationship may then be preserved over time by granting both groups similar wage increases. To our knowledge, this possibility has not been tested and thus remains purely speculative. This explanation has some intuitive appeal in that office workers are more likely to have information regarding union negotiated wage increases among manual workers in their own plant than about the relationship of white-collar to blue-collar earnings in other firms. Moreover, while their wages may be lower than those of organized white-collar workers, the latter group at present constitutes an extremely small proportion of the total (Kassalow 1967). An additional possibility is that the data are too aggregated to distinguish between situations in which the union is likely to have an impact on wage rates and those in which it is not. Important variables may include, for example, the extent of contact between the blue- and white-collar work forces and the nature of organization among blue-collar workers (i.e., industrial or craft). Raimon and Stoikov (1969) suggest that the lack of impact of blue-collar unionism is due to the greater competitiveness of clerical labor markets. However, our findings with regard to industry differences in wage rates and with regard to the impact of unionism and size of firm on wage rates in manufacturing industries are suggestive of important noncompetitive elements.

For New York and Philadelphia our findings with regard to the impact of establishment size on the dependent variables are similar to those obtained for the (plant and office) union variable. (A small but significant positive relationship between establishment size and the wage index is obtained in the Boston first regression. However, the coefficient becomes marginally insignificant when the manufacturing union variable is included. An interaction variable reflecting the joint effect of manufacturing and size was not found to be significant and thus is not reported in the second set of regressions.) In these cities the introduction of a variable reflecting the interaction of size and sector suggests that the consistent effect of large establishment size (over 1,000 employees) is mainly restricted to manufacturing (the manufacturing-size variable equals 1 if the firm is both large (over 1,000 employees) and in the manufacturing sector, and 0 otherwise). The magnitude of the manufacturing-size effect was similar in the two cities, contributing to an increase of six percentage points in the wage index in New York and nine percentage points in Philadelphia, and to a decrease of four percentage points in the proportion-female index in New York and three percentage points in Philadelphia (the last coefficient was not statistically significant).

Conclusion

In this chapter we have tested the hypotheses generated by our model concerning the wage and employment patterns of establishments. We have confirmed the existence of a wage hierarchy of firms within each labor market. The ranking of firms with respect to wage rates is shown to be consistent across occupations and sex groups. We have also demonstrated a pattern of establishment segregation that is consistent across occupational categories. Further, the ranking of establishments with respect to the representation of women was found to be inversely related to the ranking of establishments with respect to wage rates.

Our investigation of the determinants of the standing of the firm with respect to wage rates and to the representation of women in the establishment indicates that structural variables are important explanatory factors. We have noted that our results are presented with reservations in light of data problems. However, the results obtained are supportive of our model and suggest that this approach is worthy of further exploration.

Industry was found to be an important factor in the wage and proportion-female regressions. The significance of industry variables in the proportion-female regressions suggests that industry segregation does exist. Moreover, the industry coefficients were generally of opposite sign in the wage and proportion-female regressions, suggesting that the wage standing of the industry is an important factor in the interindustry variation in the representation of women.

Within the manufacturing sector, we find that unionization (of both plant and office workers) and large establishment size (over 1,000 employees) are positively related to wage rates and negatively related to the representation of women. There was no consistent pattern of the effect of these variables outside of manufacturing. This finding is deemed particularly worthy of further investigation.

Our results do not show a consistently significant relationship between the presence of a union among plant workers and either of the dependent variables. While we have offered some speculative explanations for this finding, it appears to warrant further attention.

In general the results obtained in the wage and proportion-female regression confirm our expectation that establishment characteristics that are positively related to wage rates will be negatively related to the representation of women in the establishment, and vice versa.

6 Conclusions and Recommendations

This book is concerned with the relationship of differences in the distribution of men and women office workers among firms to the male-female pay differential within narrowly defined occupational categories. The study has been designed to place at the heart of the analysis three factors which in our view have received inadequate attention in earlier empirical work.

First is the importance of distributional differences in explaining pay differentials by sex. While a growing number of scholars have focused attention on the differential distribution of men and women among occupational categories as a principal explanatory factor in male-female earnings differences, empirical work in this area has been largely concerned with with the measurement of wage discrimination. The general practice has been to estimate what proportion of the male-female pay differential is attributable to differences in the productivity-related characteristics of male and female workers, and to ascribe the residual (unexplained) portion of the differential to discrimination. The impact of distributional differences, whether implicitly included in the estimate of wage discrimination or removed through controls for detailed occupational categories, is seldom given a central place in the analysis. We have endeavored to develop a unified analysis of the relationship of distributional differences along one dimension (among firms) to pay differentials within occupations.

Second is the importance of the establishment as a decision-making unit in the economy. Studies in this area have generally taken the individual as the unit of analysis, thus focusing on the supply side of the problem. By taking the establishment as the unit of analysis, we are able to examine the data at the level of disaggregation, where many of the employment decisions that produce the observed patterns of employment segregation and pay differentials are made. While this is a more demand-oriented approach, adjustments are made for important supply factors, particularly the occupation and skill level of workers which are proxies for labor quality.

A third and related point is the role of institutional and market factors in constraining the latitude of the employer to differentiate between male and female workers. Analyses of employer discrimination generally proceed from an assumption of perfect competition in the labor market. We believe that the role of employer preferences can best be understood within a framework that takes explicit account of the institutional and market constraints under which employers operate. The institutional approach employed here is the internal labor market analysis. This framework was derived primarily from the study of blue-collar labor markets. Thus the empirical verification of our model constitutes a test of the applicability of a model derived from these sources to office workers, as well as a test of the usefulness of such an approach for the analysis of employment segregation and sex differentials in wages. The model is tested with a sample of clerical, professional, and technical occupations in three large northeastern labor markets: Boston, New York, and Philadelphia. It is our view that the model performs well on both counts, and is deserving of further application with other data sets.

In this chapter, a summary and overview of the study is presented and the policy implications of the findings are discussed. The existing legal remedies to the problems investigated in the study are then summarized and evaluated. Finally our own proposals for a more effective approach to altering women's employment status are presented. The need for a consolidation of the enforcement efforts in the employment-rights area, for increased cooperation of unions in this effort, and for more favorable macroeconomic policies is emphasized.

Summary and Overview of Findings

The major findings of the study are summarized in this section. First, the basic framework used in the study, the internal labor market analysis, is reviewed, and the implications of this approach for an understanding of sex discrimination in the labor market are discussed. Second, the extent of sex-segregation by occupation in the labor market is detailed, since such segregation provides the aggregate labor market context in which distributional differences between men and women in the same occupational categories occur. Third, the application of the internal labor market approach to an analysis of pay differences between men and women in the same occupational categories is explained, and the consistency of our empirical findings with this conceptual framework is examined. Fourth, the issue of the relative importance of demand- and supply-side factors in producing the observed inequalities between men and women in the labor market is considered. Finally, the implications for anti-discrimination policies of our approach and empirical findings are presented.

Internal Labor Market Analysis

The internal labor market analysis involves seeing the job structure of the firm as divided into two types of occupations. First are those job categories that are filled from sources external to the firm through the recruitment of new workers. Within clusters of related occupations, such entry jobs are generally restricted to lower-level positions. Second are those job categories that are filled from internal sources through advancement up well-defined promotion ladders. The process by which workers advance from entry-level positions to higher-level jobs is conceptualized as one in which they acquire, either formally or informally, added knowledge or skills that are to some significant extent firm specific.

The requirement of enterprise-specific skills for the performance of internally allocated jobs works to prevent the development of a competitive market (in the traditional sense) for these categories of occupations and widens the range of administrative influence within the firm. An internal labor market develops, that is, an administrative apparatus that allocates labor and determines wage rates within the firm. Thus the internal labor market structure may be seen as specifying a relatively rigid set of wage relationships and promotional possibilities, both of which are defined primarily in terms of job categories. The wage relationships among individuals and the promotional possibilities for any given individual are for the most part established as a consequence of workers' job assignments in the firm.

Two points of this analysis are particularly relevant to an understanding of sex discrimination in the labor market. The first point sheds light on the motive for such discrimination and the second on the form which such discrimination may be expected to take.

First, within the internal labor market, group or categorical treatment of individuals is the norm. Such group treatment will be more efficient (result in the discarding of less information) the greater the degree of intragroup homogeneity with respect to whatever characteristics are considered important. Thus statistical discrimination is likely to play an important role in rationing job opportunities in such a situation. If employers believe women are less stable workers than men, sex will be an obvious basis for differentiation among workers. Of course, employer distaste for hiring women or male employees' distaste for working with women could provide further incentives for differential treatment.

Second, within the internal labor market framework, segregation is the form discrimination may be expected to take and the mechanism by which pay differentials are produced because segregation is the primary way in which employers can differentiate between men and women, even with respect to wage rates. Under the constraints imposed by the administered system of the internal labor market, the latitude of the employer to differentiate among individuals (or between sex groups) is relatively broad with respect to hiring and job allocation. It is considerably narrower with respect to wage differentiation among individuals within the same job (unequal pay for equal work) and with respect to the alteration of wage relationships among occupational categories.

Thus employers may exclude women from certain entry-level positions and their associated promotion ladders or promote and upgrade women more slowly than men. Indeed the very structure of the jobs typically open to women is likely to reflect employer perceptions regarding the average characteristics of female workers. Predominantly female occupations may be characterized by fewer possibilities for promotion and more numerous ports of entry than comparable male jobs—the source of the common complaint that women's jobs are dead-end jobs. To the extent that exclusion occurs, it is likely to produce segregation both by occupation and, within occupations, by firm. In both cases, male-female pay differentials are likely to be associated with the restricted access of women to higher-paying opportunities. The primary concern in this study has been with sex-segregation by firm within occupational categories. However, from a policy point of view, the magnitude of sex segregation by occupation is also extremely important, and so this has also been examined.

Sex-Segregation by Occupation

The investigation of the extent of segregation by occupation reveals the the existence of a substantial amount of this type of segregation in the labor market, as well as a relative stability in its magnitude over the twenty-year period from 1950 to 1970. The measure of segregation by occupation used in the study indicates that in each census year roughly two-thirds of the female (or male) labor force would have had to change occupations for the occupational distribution of the two groups to be the same or, equivalently, for the representation of women in each occupational category to equal the representation of women in the total labor force. While a small reduction in the degree of segregation by occupation appears to have occurred between 1960 and 1970, it appears to be explicable in terms of changes in the structure of the economy that caused a drop in the proportion of men employed in highly segregated (0-10 percent female) occupations. The declining relative importance of agricultural work, unskilled labor, and self-employment was identified as the major factor responsible for the movement of men out of this group of occupations. At the same time, the rapid growth in many predominantly female jobs, particularly in the clerical category, permitted the absorption of increasing numbers of women into the labor force, even in the absence of a redistribution of women workers towards predominantly male or integrated occupations.

Thus it appears that the segregation of men and women by occupation provides the labor-market context in which differences in the distribution of men and women by firm within occupational categories occur. In fact the predominantly single-sex occupational work group is the norm in the economy, and sex differences in the distribution of employment among firms may be seen as a further dimension of labor-market segregation.

Internal Labor Market Analysis: An Application

As we stated earlier, the segregation of men and women by firm is analyzed within a model which takes explicit account of the institutional and market constraints on employer behavior. Two types of constraints are identified from the literature associated with the internal labor market analysis.

First are institutional considerations internal to the firm that place limits on the employer's ability to differentiate among individuals (and thus between men and women). In particular, the employer is seen as being constrained to pay the same base pay rate to all workers within an occupational category. Wage differentiation among individuals within occupational categories is limited to seniority and merit considerations. In addition, the employer faces a relatively rigid internal wage structure which specifies wage relationships among occupational categories.

Second are institutional and market considerations which determine the position of the establishment in the labor-market wage hierarchy. Given the interrelationships among occupational wage rates and the necessity of equal base occupational pay rates by sex, the relative wage position of the firm is postulated as being consistent across related occupational categories and sex groups.

These factors operate on the demand side to yield a structure of occupational wage rates that may be offered by the firm, regardless of the sex of the worker employed. The wage relationships specified by the internal wage structure and the position of the firm in the wage hierarchy of establishments are shaped by a variety of factors and cannot easily be altered to accommodate employer preferences regarding the sex composition of specific occupational categories. It is argued that, while the preference for male over female labor is fairly widespread, the ability to exercise this preference is constrained by the position of the firm in the wage hierarchy. Thus, in each occupational category, male workers are primarily sought by and attracted to the higher-wage establishments, while female workers, for the most part, find employment in the lower-paying firms which, regardless of their preferences, are less able to compete for male labor. Since the wage standing of the firm is postulated as being consistent across occupational categories and sex groups, the model predicts consistent establishment-wide patterns with respect to the representation of women across occupational categories.

The major findings of the study are supportive of this model. At the level of the occupational category it is found that men and women are differentially distributed among firms to a degree in excess of what could be expected from the operation of random processes, confirming the existence of sex segregation by firm within occupational categories. Further, this differential distribution is found to be an important factor in the sex differential in earnings. For the most part, earnings differentials by sex within occupations are primarily the result of differences in pay rates among firms rather than differences in pay rates within firms.

The causal mechanism postulated by the model is further verified by examining occupations jointly to form a picture of establishment wage and employment patterns. We demonstrate the existence of a wage hierarchy of firms within each labor market that is consistent across occupational categories and sex groups. In addition, after controlling for the occupational mix of the establishment (and thus the differing availability of women to the firm in each occupational category), we find that firms exhibit consistent patterns across occupational categories with respect to the representation of women. And, as expected, the wage standing of the firm is found to be inversely related to the representation of women in the establishment.

The relationship of establishment characteristics (industry, union status, and size of firm) to interfirm differences in wage rates and in the representation of women is also explored. The results are offered somewhat tentatively because of a variety of data problems. However, our findings suggest that structural variables are important for explaining the observed differences among firms in wage rates and the sex composition of establishment employment. In general it is found that variables that are positively related to establishment wage rates are negatively related to the representation of women in the establishment, and vice versa. In particular, industry is found to be an important explanatory factor in both cases, suggesting that the sexes are differentially distributed by industry and that such segregation is related to the wage standing of firms within the industry.

One of the more interesting findings in the investigation of the determinants of interfirm differences in wage rates and employment patterns is that the consistent effect of (plant and office worker) unionization and of large firm size (over 1,000 employees) appears to be restricted to the manufacturing sector. Within manufacturing industries, these variables are positively associated with the wage standing of the establishment and negatively associated with the representation of women in the firm. With respect to the impact of blue-collar unionism on the wage rates of unorganized white-collar workers, our findings are consistent with the results obtained in other studies—that there appears to be no significant relationship.

Demand, Supply and the Interdependence of Demand and Supply

The view presented here is that demand-side factors play an important role in generating male-female pay differentials within occupational categories. Such differentials are seen as primarily the result of differences in the distribution of men and women among establishments stemming from the exclusionary practices of higher-wage firms. It is argued on the basis of theoretical considerations and empirical evidence that measured pay differentials among firms generally exceed differences that may reasonably be attributed to exogenously determined quality differences among workers (i.e., supply-side factors). Further, it is argued that worker quality is relatively homogeneous within the detailed occupational categories used in the analysis. However, in the absence of additional data on the personal characteristics of workers we do not attempt to measure and quantify the impact of discrimination on pay differentials in specific cases. Rather, we are concerned with delineating the broad pattern of the relationship between pay differentials and distributional differences, observed across a variety of occupational categories. In addition, the results obtained when occupations are considered separately are linked to consistent establishment-wide patterns, again suggesting that demand-side factors are important. The results of this study suggest that demand-side factors produce pay differentials and employment segregation even when men and women have similar skills and abilities as evinced by their participation in the same narrowly defined occupational categories.

While it is not an easy matter to separate demand- from supply-side factors when considering pay and employment distribution differences between men and women employed in the same occupations, it is even more difficult to do so when considering the aggregate pay differential and the segregation of men and women by occupation.[1] Considerable evidence of the importance of demand-side factors is available, in that most empirical studies trace a substantial proportion of the male-female pay differential to discrimination (Sawhill 1973). However, given the interdependence of discrimination on the demand side and the supply characteristics of those experiencing discrimination, an attempt to separate definitively the effects of the two may not prove fruitful. This interdependence is well summarized by Barbara Bergmann:

some proportion of whatever differences in abilities by race and sex there are results from the effect of discrimination by employers on the development and expression of abilities in the individuals adversely affected. The restrictive hiring, pay and promotion practices which employers have applied to blacks and women have inevitably affected the education, training, attitudes, and labor force attachment of the people economically hobbled by such practices (Bergmann 1976, p. 127).

Such an assessment suggests that the consequences of labor-market discrimination may be both difficult to measure and far-reaching. However, it also implies that effective policies to end labor-market discrimination may also have far-reaching effects, particularly when combined with simultaneous changes in social attitudes towards women's roles. A diminution in labor-market discrimination may be expected to have "ripple effects," as the equalization of market incentives between the sexes induces further changes in women's supply-side decisions. In addition, as more women enter previously male-dominated fields, ripple effects may be expected to result from the greater availability of role models for younger women. Thus demand-side policies can be expected to play an important role in initiating and sustaining a process of cumulative change in women's economic status. The findings of this study suggest certain broad guidelines for such policies.

Policy Implications

The results obtained in this study strongly suggest that segregation by firm is at the root of sex differences in earnings within occupational categories. When viewed in combination with the evidence of the large magnitude of segregation of men and women by occupation, our findings suggest that higher priority should be given to increasing the access of women to a broader range of job opportunities (reducing the extent of employment segregation by sex) than to enforcing equal pay for equal work within the firm.

It is important that policy measures designed to reduce sex segregation in the labor market take into account the depth and dimensions of such segregation. Not only are men and women segregated by occupational categories, but within occupational categories they are segregated by establishment and industry. Moreover, our findings indicate that the differences in the distribution of men and women among firms is not limited to a small group of relatively prestigious occupations. Rather, such segregation by firm is seen to be a pervasive characteristic of female employment within a wide range of white-collar occupations, including categories in which women predominate. Thus efforts to ensure equal access of women to establishments must be aimed at an equally wide range of occupations.

Our analysis also suggests that efforts to integrate presently segregated occupational categories must operate on the demand as well as the supply side if they are to be effective in reducing aggregate pay differentials by sex. Thus it is not sufficient simply to advocate the integration of presently segregated occupations through changes in the supply characteristics of women. The forces on the demand side must also be combatted. Otherwise it is likely that, as women enter formerly male-dominated areas, they will continue to be segregated, in this case by establishment.

The internal labor market analysis that has been employed in this study also has important policy implications as it sheds light on the nature of discrimination women are likely to encounter. Much of the discrimination against women may be characterized as institutional or systemic in nature, resulting from the class or group treatment of women. The pattern-or-practice approach is probably the most effective way to attack discrimination of this type. The existence of institutional sex discrimination on the part of a firm can be inferred from such factors as the degree of utilization of women by the firm in comparison to their availability in each occupation in the labor market, the extent of sex segregation by occupation within the firm, the pay rates and the promotion opportunities associated with predominantly female as compared with predominantly male job categories, and sex differences in promotion rates when men and women are employed in the same classifications. In many cases, such pattern-and-practice charges are easier to substantiate and document than are allegations of discrimination against a particular individual. In addition, a larger number of women would be affected by the successful resolution of a pattern-and-practice charge than of an individual complaint. Thus for a variety of reasons it appears that the pattern-and-practice approach should play a major role in the enforcement of anti-discrimination policies.

In pursuing the pattern-and-practice strategy, our findings suggest that a higher priority in enforcement be given to larger firms and unionized establishments. Within manufacturing, it was found that, other things equal, such firms pay higher wages and employ fewer women. In addition, concentrating resources on the larger firms ensures that a larger number of individuals are affected in each case.

In addition, an effective antidiscrimination effort must include a clear and consistent enunciation of the government policy in this area, coupled with timely and uniform enforcement of this policy. These elements of an enforcement effort are important not only to ensure that transgressors are brought to justice and that the victims of discrimination are compensated: since sex discrimination is so pervasive, it is at least equally important that the enforcement effort stimulate voluntary compliance on the part of the majority of employers. This is likely to occur only if the government policies are readily comprehensible, if the steps necessary to comply with the laws and regulations in this area are clear, and if there is a reasonably high probability that noncompliance will result in sanctions.

Legal Remedies: Employment Legislation

At present there exists an impressive array of laws and regulations prohibiting sex discrimination in employment. (See *Exploitation from 9 to 5* (1975, pp. 87-113, 145-47) for a detailed summary of such legislation.)

The *Equal Pay Act of 1963* prohibits differential pay rates for men and women who perform substantially equal work in the same establishment, where equal work is defined as work requiring equal skill, effort, and responsibility and which is performed under similar working conditions. The Equal Pay Act is enforced by the wage and hour division of the Department of Labor.

Title VII of the Civil Rights Act of 1964 prohibits employers from discriminating in hiring or firing, compensation, terms, conditions or privileges of employment, and employer-provided training. Employment agencies, labor organizations and joint labor management committees are also prohibited from discriminating on the basis of sex. Exceptions to Title VII may be permitted when sex is found to be a bona fide occupational qualification. The enforcement powers of the Equal Employment Opportunity Commission (EEOC) which administers the act were initially limited to conciliation and to filing friend of the court briefs in private suits. However, since 1972 the EEOC has been empowered to file in federal district court against offenders (with the exception of government agencies for which this power resides with the Justice Department). In addition, since 1974 the EEOC has been empowered to bring pattern-and-practice actions; formerly this was the responsibility of the attorney general.

Executive Order 11246 prohibits sex discrimination on the part of federal contractors and subcontractors, including those doing federally assisted construction, in all their facilities. In addition, contractors are required to take affirmative action to insure equal employment opportunity. The Office of Federal Contract Compliance (OFCC) of the Department of Labor has the overall responsibility for enforcement and consistent application of the executive order. The compliance program is administered by sixteen contract-compliance agencies on an industry-wide basis (e.g., the Treasury Department for the finance industry). Noncomplying employers face possible suspension or cancellation of their government contracts.

Title IX of the Educational Amendments of 1972 prohibits sex discrimination against employees and students in federally assisted educational programs, including educational institutions that receive federal assistance. Title IX is enforced by the Office for Civil Rights of the Department of Health, Education and Welfare. This agency is empowered to delay or cancel government awards in the case of noncompliance and to request that the Department of Justice bring suit against offending educational institutions.

An Evaluation

The existing federal legislation and regulations prohibit a wide range of discriminatory practices on the part of employers. In addition to forbidding discrimination on the demand side, federal legislation impacts on the supply side of the problem through Title IX's ban on discrimination against women students. Moreover, the existing case law in the equal-employment-opportunity area tends to support relatively stringent interpretations of the provisions of the law. For example, both the EEOC and the major court decisions have taken the view that the bona fide occupation-qualification exception to Title VII should be interpreted narrowly, that is, individuals are entitled to consideration on the basis of individual capabilities and not on the basis of characteristics generally attributed to the group.[2] Nor can sex in combination with some other factor be used as a legal basis for discrimination under Title VII. The courts have held, for example, that an employer cannot refuse to hire women with preschool age children while men with preschool age children are hired.[3]

Nonetheless, there is widespread disaffection with the federal effort to end employment discrimination, and a major study by the United States Commission on Civil Rights concluded that this effort is "fundamentally inadequate" (1975, vol. 5, p. i). Most of the agencies charged with enforcement are underfinanced and understaffed, and the processing of complaints is characterized by backlogs and delays. For example, although the coverage of the Equal Pay Act was broadened in 1972 to include a large number of workers who were originally exempt from the act, the number of Department of Labor compliance officers charged with investigating violations of the act has not increased significantly since 1963 (U.S. Commission on Civil Rights 1975, vol. 5, p. 639). The enforcement of Title VII is plagued by even greater difficulties. The EEOC's backlog now includes 120,000 pending cases with a 2-7-year waiting period for processing (*The Spokeswoman*, vol. 6, 1976, p. 5).

However more fundamental problems exist in the present situation, stemming from the fragmentation of the antidiscrimination-enforcement effort into the domains of a variety of agencies. As the U.S. Commission on Civil Rights noted, "There is no one person, agency, or institution which can speak for the Federal Government in this important area. Thus, employers, employees, and aggrieved citizens are left to their own devices in trying to understand and react to a complex administrative structure (U.S. Commission on Civil Rights 1975, vol. 5, p. 617). The result is a variety of difficulties.

First, there is a great deal of overlapping coverage in the laws and regulations administered by the various agencies, leading to duplication of effort and waste of resources. In addition, inconsistency in enforcement may result from conflicting interpretations and requirements of the agencies. For example, there is a serious disagreement among the wage- and hour-administrator, OFCC, and EEOC with respect to the requirements for nondiscriminatory fringe benefits, specifically, to the issue of whether equal benefits to employees or equal contributions by employers are required (Wallace 1976, pp. 131-32). Problems may be present even with respect to the enforcement effort of one agency. For example, since the OFCC delegates enforcement authority to contract compliance agencies, different agencies may assert jurisdiction over the same contractors (U.S. Commission on Civil Rights 1975, vol. 5, p. 634).

Second, the involvement of various agencies makes it difficult to set uniform priorities in the allocation of resources for enforcement. Thus far, no clear set of priorities has emerged either for the division of labor among agencies, or the internal policies of each agency with respect to the relative importance to be given such approaches as enforcing equal pay for equal work rather than enforcing equal employment opportunities (equal access), prosecuting individual complaints rather than pattern and practice charges, investigating the employment practices of small rather than large enterprises.

Third, the current structure appears to militate against uniform and timely enforcement of the law. Under the present system, it is possible that some employers will be deluged by investigators from different agencies, subjected to conflicting compliance requirements, and forced to defend themselves against the same discrimination charge in a seemingly endless number of forums. Other employers (one suspects the majority) may not be subjected to any serious pressure to conform to the antidiscrimination statutes and regulations. At the same time, victims of discrimination languish as their complaints remain unprocessed.

Fourth, it is very difficult to make such an administrative network accountable to the public and, most importantly, to those groups whose rights it is responsible for upholding. For example, in mid-August 1976, the EEOC announced new regulations to reduce the backlog of charges filed before 1974 (*The Spokeswoman*, vol. 7, 1975, p. 5). A month later, the United States Department of Labor proposed new regulations for enforcement of the Executive Order 11246 (*The Spokeswoman*, vol. 7, 1976, p. 1). In both cases, civil rights groups had serious objections to the changes. The burden of keeping informed about and attempting to influence a number of agencies can only attenuate the impact of a concerned public on policies in this area.

A Strategy for Change

We propose a strategy for change in women's economic status that includes an overhaul of the antidiscrimination enforcement apparatus, an increased role for labor unions, and a greater emphasis on full employment.

Enforcement of Anti-Discrimination Policies

The proposal by the United States Commission on Civil Rights for the establishment of a consolidated agency—the National Employment Rights Board (NERB)—with broad powers to enforce a single antibias statute (U.S. Commission on Civil Rights 1975, vol. 5, p. 649) appears to be the most sensible solution to the enforcement difficulties detailed in the previous section. The powers of such an agency, its organization, priorities, and approach should be determined only after careful study and ample input from concerned parties. In an effort to contribute to the policy discussion, we present our own suggestions concerning these matters.

Impacting the Labor Market: The Pattern and Practice Approach. As noted earlier, the pattern-and-practice approach should be given high priority in the enforcement of antidiscrimination policies. We here propose an implementation procedure.

It is proposed that information be collected annually on the utilization of women by firms (such information is currently collected by the EEOC). A group of firms with poor performance records could be identified on the basis of two criteria: the representation of women in the major occupational categories in the firm in comparison with their availability in the labor market, and the extent of improvement over the previous year. A random sample of firms from the poor performance group could then be selected for investigation. Before sampling, the firms may be classified by size so that the cost of the investigations can be accurately forecast and so that, if desired, priority may be given to larger firms.

This procedure has the advantage of encouraging voluntary compliance because improvement is taken into account in the selection of firms for investigation.

Eliminating the Backlog: Individual Complaints. While it is important to give priority to the pattern-and-practice cases that have the largest impact, the complaints of individuals cannot be ignored. Complaints brought by individuals may raise important legal issues with potentially far-reaching effects. In addition, the existing antidiscrimination legislation and regulations have given rise to expectations that the rights of individuals to nondiscriminatory treatment in employment would be protected. Indeed it is difficult to conceive of an effective enforcement policy that did not include the guarantee of individual rights.

Efforts to ensure individuals their rights have thus far foundered in their inability to process the large number of complaints that have been generated. The processing of such complaints must be expedited if the guarantee of individual rights is to be meaningful. Individuals seeking a relatively small amount of damages (e.g., under $2,000) are particularly in need of assistance since they are unlikely to be able to obtain private counsel, even on a contingency fee basis.

In such cases, a mechanism is needed for providing equitable relief to individuals, preferably in a relatively informal setting where parties need not be represented by counsel. There now exists a number of models of small dispute resolution that might be adapted to employment rights cases, including small claims courts, administrative hearings, and compulsory arbitration of tort cases. We propose that the alternative models be studied and that the most promising approach be adopted, so that the processing of individual complaints may be expedited.

Funding and Performance. Regardless of the reforms that are eventually made in the present administrative apparatus, it is absolutely essential that adequate funding be provided for an anti-discrimination policy to be effectual. In addition, it is important that the performance of the agency or agencies charged with ensuring equal employment opportunity be constantly monitored to see that they do indeed carry out that charge.

The Role of Unions

Labor unions have a growing interest in the equal employment opportunity area as well as an important contribution to make. The unions' interest in taking a more active role in the employment rights area is based on two considerations. First, union membership as a share of nonagricultural employment has been stagnating in recent years. For example, union members accounted for 33 percent of nonagricultural employment in 1956 as compared to 27 percent in

1970 (Reynolds 1974, p. 368). If the union movement is to grow, it is necessary that it make inroads into sectors of the labor force where women comprise a relatively high proportion of workers, including white-collar workers and public employees. Thus unions have a stake in making membership more attractive to women. Second, recent court decisions suggest that unions may face financial liability for back pay and legal-fee judgments if they do not take a more active role in combatting discrimination. Even industrial unions that do not exercise control over hiring may face liability to the extent that they acquiesce in employment practices that perpetuate discrimination (Hammerman and Rogoff 1976, p. 34).

The potential contribution of labor unions to equal employment opportunity is large. First, the union grievance machinery and arbitration may be the most expeditious means to resolve many simple (single-issue) employment discrimination cases, particularly those involving alleged violation of the union contract (Edwards 1976, pp. 265, 273). The successful resolution of some discrimination cases through this process would help to reduce the task of federal enforcement agencies. Second, collective bargaining offers a means of eliminating discriminatory practices as well as a means of raising demands that could have an impact on women's economic status, including, for example, the provision of child care, the introduction of flexitime, and a decline in the standard work day or work week.

A Call for Full Employment

A discussion of a strategy for altering women's economic status would hardly be complete without some consideration of the impact of the level of unemployment on women. The adverse effect on women of periods of high unemployment cannot be overemphasized. First, since the unemployment rate of women is generally higher than that of men, women bear a disproportionate share of unemployment. Second, in times of high unemployment, many women become discouraged and drop out of the labor force, while others postpone their entry until economic conditions improve. Thus, "hidden unemployment" is a particular problem for women. Finally, and perhaps more importantly, the level of unemployment will undoubtedly affect the social acceptance of programs designed to increase the opportunities for women in what are presently predominantly male jobs.

An unavoidable consequence of the effort to expand the employment opportunities open to women is that men will face a new source of competition. Thus some men may find that they are unable to obtain employment in their preferred occupation or firm. However, under conditions of full employment, they can find employment elsewhere. Further, buoyant demand conditions combined with a new mobility for women workers would tend to reduce earnings differentials among jobs that were once predominantly male or female. Thus the price paid by men for being unable to obtain their first choice may not prove to be very great. On the other hand, during periods of high unemployment, public support for a fundamental change in women's employment status is likely to diminish. Moreover, since it is the new jobs that become available in a growing, healthy economy that are most likely to become open to women, the maintenance of full employment is important if we are to move rapidly toward the goal of economic equality for women.

Appendix A
Occupational Descriptions

The following are detailed occupational descriptions for the office, professional, and technical jobs included in this study.[1] These descriptions have been prepared by the Bureau of Labor Statistics primarily to assist its field staff in classifying workers who are employed under a variety of payroll titles and work arrangements from establishment to establishment and area to area. In each case, field staff exclude working supervisors, apprentices, learners, beginners, trainees, and handicapped; also excluded are part-time, temporary, and probationary workers.

Office Occupations

Biller, Machine

Prepares statements, bills, and invoices on a machine other than an ordinary or electromatic typewriter. May also keep records as to billings or shipping charges or perform other clerical work incidental to billing operations. Machine billers are classified by type of machine, as follows:

> *Biller, machine (billing machine).* Uses a special billing machine (Moon Hopkins, Elliott Fisher, Burroughs, etc., which are combination typing and adding machines) to prepare bills and invoices from customers' purchase orders, internally prepared orders, shipping memorandums, etc. Usually involves application of predetermined discounts and shipping charges, and entry of necessary extensions, which may or may not be computed on the billing machine, and totals, which are automatically accumulated by machine. The operation usually involves a large number of carbon copies of the bill being prepared and is often done on a fanfold machine.

> *Biller, machine (bookkeeping machine).* Uses a bookkeeping machine (Sundstrand, Elliott Fisher, Remington Rand, etc., which may or may not have typewriter keyboard) to prepare customers' bills as part of the accounts-receivable operation. Generally involves the simultaneous entry of figures on customers' ledger record. The machine automatically accumulates figures on a number of vertical columns and computes, and usually prints automatically, the debit or credit balances. Does not involve a knowledge of bookkeeping. Works from uniform and standard types of sales and credit slips.

Bookkeeping-Machine Operator

Operates a bookkeeping machine (Remington Rand, Elliott Fisher, Sundstrand, Burroughs, National Cash Register, with or without a typewriter keyboard) to keep a record of business transactions.

113

Class A. Keeps a set of records requiring a knowledge of and experience in basic bookkeeping principles, and familiarity with the structure of the particular accounting system used. Determines proper records and distribution of debit and credit items to be used in each phase of the work. May prepare consolidated reports, balance sheets, and other records by hand.

Class B. Keeps a record of one or more phases or sections of a set of records usually requiring little knowledge of basic bookkeeping. Phases or sections include accounts payable, payroll, customers' accounts (not including a simple type of billing described under "biller, machine"), cost distribution, expense distribution, inventory control, etc. May check or assist in preparation of trial balances and prepare control sheets for the accounting department.

Clerk, Accounting

Class A. Under general direction of a bookkeeper or accountant, has responsibility for keeping one or more sections of a complete set of books or records relating to one phase of an establishment's business transactions. Work involves posting and balancing subsidiary ledger or ledgers such as accounts receivable or accounts payable, examining and coding invoices or vouchers with proper accounting distribution, and requires judgment and experience in making proper assignations and allocations. May assist in preparing, adjusting, and closing journal entries, and may direct class B accounting clerks.

Class B. Under supervision, performs one or more routine accounting operations such as posting simple journal vouchers or accounts payable vouchers, entering vouchers in voucher registers, reconciling bank accounts, and posting subsidiary ledgers controlled by general ledgers or posting simple cost-accounting data. This job does not require a knowledge of accounting and bookkeeping principles but is found in offices in which the more routine accounting work is subdivided on a functional basis among several workers.

Clerk, File

Class A. In an established filing system containing a number of varied subject-matter files, classifies and indexes file material such as correspondence, reports, technical documents, etc. May also file this material, keep records of various types in conjunction with the files, may lead a small group of lower-level file clerks.

Class B. Sorts, codes, and files unclassified material by simple (subject-matter) headings or partly classified material by finer subheadings. Prepares a simple related index and cross-reference aids. As requested, locates clearly identified material in files and forwards material. May perform related clerical tasks required to maintain and service files.

Class C. Performs routine filing of material that has already been classified or which is easily classified in a simple serial-classification system (e.g., alphabetical, chronological, or numerical). As requested, locates readily available material in files and forwards material, and may fill out withdrawal charge. Performs simple clerical and manual tasks required to maintain and service files.

Clerk, Order

Receives customers' orders for material or merchandise by mail, phone, or personally. Duties involve any combination of the following: quoting prices to customers, making out an order sheet listing the items to make up the order, checking prices and quantities of items on order sheet, and distributing order sheets to respective departments to be filled. May check with credit department to determine credit rating of customer, acknowledge receipt of orders from customers, follow up orders to see that they have been filled, keep file of orders received, and check shipping invoices with original orders.

Clerk, Payroll

Computes wages of company employees and enters the necessary data on the payroll sheets. Duties involve calculating workers' earnings based on time or production records and posting calculated data on payroll sheet, showing information such as worker's name, working days, time, rate, deductions for insurance, and total wages due. May make out paychecks and assist paymaster in making up and distributing pay envelopes. May use a calculating machine.

Comptometer Operator

Primary duty is to operate a Comptometer to perform mathematical computations. This job is not to be confused with that of statistical or other type of clerk, which may involve frequent use of a Comptometer but in which use of this machine is incidental to performance of other duties.

Keypunch Operator

Class A. Operates a numerical and/or alphabetical or combination keypunch machine to transcribe data from various source documents to keypunch tabulating cards. Performs same tasks as lower-level keypunch operator but, in addition, work requires application of coding skills and the making of some determinations, for example, locates on the source document the items to be punched, extracts information from several documents, and searches for and interprets information on the document to determine information to be punched. May train inexperienced operators.

116

Class B. Under close supervision or following specific procedures or instructions, transcribes data from source documents to punched cards. Operates a numerical and/or alphabetical or combination keypunch machine to keypunch tabulating cards. May verify cards. Working from various standardized source documents, follows specified sequences which have been coded or prescribed in detail and require little or no selecting, coding, or interpreting of data to be punched. Problems arising from erroneous items or codes, missing information, etc., are referred to supervisor.

Office Boy or Girl

Performs various routine duties such as running errands, operating minor office machines such as sealers or mailers, opening and distributing mail, and other minor clerical work.

Secretary

Assigned as personal secretary, normally to one individual. Maintains a close and highly responsive relationship to the day-to-day work activities of the supervisor. Works fairly independently receiving a minimum of detailed supervision and guidance. Performs varied clerical and secretarial duties, usually including most of the following: receives telephone calls, personal callers, and incoming mail, answers routine inquiries, and routes the technical inquiries to the proper persons; establishes, maintains, and revises the supervisor's files; maintains the supervisor's calendar and makes appointments as instructed; relays messages from supervisor to subordinates; review correspondence, memoranda, and reports prepared by others for the supervisor's signature to assure procedural and typographic accuracy; and performs stenographic and typing work.

May also perform other clerical and secretarial work of comparable nature and difficulty. The work typically requires knowledge of office routine and understanding of the organization, programs, and procedures related to the work of the supervisor.

Exclusions. Not all positions that are titled *secretary* possess the above characteristics. Examples of positions which are excluded from the definition are as follows: positions which do not meet the personal secretary concept described above; stenographers not fully trained in secretarial-type duties; stenographers serving as office assistants to a group of professional, technical, or managerial persons; secretary positions in which the duties are either substantially more routine or substantially more complex and responsible than those characterized in the definition; and assistant-type positions which involve more difficult or more responsible technical, administrative, supervisory, or specialized clerical duties which are not typical of secretarial work.

Note: The term *corporate officer* used in the level definitions following, refers to those officials who have a significant corporatewide policy-making role with regard to major company activities. The title *vice president*, though normally indicative of this role, does not in all cases identify such positions. Vice presidents whose primary responsibility is to act personally on individual cases or transactions (e.g., approve or deny individual loan or credit actions, administer individual trust accounts, directly supervise a clerical staff) are not considered to be corporate officers for purposes of applying the following level definitions.

Class A.1. Secretary to the chairman of the board or president of a company that employs, in all, over 100 but fewer than 5,000 persons; or

Class A.2. Secretary to a corporate officer (other than the chairman of the board or president) of a company that employs, in all, over 5,000 but fewer than 25,000 persons; or

Class A.3. Secretary to the head (immediately below the corporate officer level) of a major segment or subsidiary of a company that employs, in all, over 25,000 persons.

Class B.1. Secretary to the chairman of the board or president of a company that employs, in all, fewer than 100 persons; or

Class B.2. Secretary to a corporate officer (other than the chairman of the board or president) of a company that employs, in all, over 100 but fewer than 5,000 persons; or

Class B.3. Secretary to the head (immediately below the officer level) of either a major corporatewide functional activity (e.g., marketing, research, operations, industrial relations, etc.) or a major geographic or organizational segment (e.g., a regional headquarters, a major division) of a company that employs, in all, over 5,000 but fewer than 25,000 employees; or

Class B.4. Secretary to the head of an individual plant, factory, etc. (or other equivalent level of official) that employs, in all, over 5,000 persons; or

Class B.5. Secretary to the head of a large and important organizational segment (e.g., a middle management supervisor of an organizational segment often involving as many as several hundred persons) of a company that employs, in all, over 25,000 persons.

Class C.1. Secretary to an executive or managerial person whose responsibility is not equivalent to one of the specific level situations in the definition for class B, but whose subordinate staff normally numbers at least several dozen employees and is usually divided into organizational segments which are often, in turn, further subdivided. In some companies, this level includes a wide range of organizational echelons, in others, only one or two; or

Class C.2. Secretary to the head of an individual plant, factory, etc. (or other equivalent level of official) that employs, in all, fewer than 5,000 persons.

Class D.1. Secretary to the supervisor or head of a *small* organizational unit (e.g., fewer than about 25 or 30 persons); or

Class D.2. Secretary to a nonsupervisory staff specialist, professional employee, administrative officer, or assistant, skilled technician, or expert. (Many companies assign stenographers, rather than secretaries as described above, to this level of supervisory or nonsupervisory worker.)

Stenographer, General

Primary duty is to take dictation involving a normal routine vocabulary from one or more persons either in shorthand or by Stenotype or similar machine, and transcribe dictation. May also type from written copy. May maintain files, keep simple records, or perform other relatively routine clerical tasks. May operate from a stenographic pool. Does not include transcribing-machine work. (See transcribing-machine operator.)

Stenographer, Senior

Primary duty is to take dictation involving a varied technical or specialized vocabulary such as in legal briefs or reports on scientific research from one or more persons either in shorthand or by Stenotype or similar machine, and transcribe dictation. May also type from written copy. May also set up and maintain files, keep records, etc., or

Performs stenographic duties requiring significantly greater independence and responsibility than stenographers, general as evidenced by the following: work requires high degree of stenographic speed and accuracy and a thorough working knowledge of general business and office procedures and of the specific business operations, organization, policies, procedures, files, workflow, etc. Uses this knowledge in performing stenographic duties and responsible clerical tasks such as maintaining followup files, assembling material for reports, memorandums, letters, etc., composing simple letters from general instructions, reading and routing incoming mail, and answering routine questions, etc. Does not include transcribing-machine work.

Switchboard Operator

Class A. Operates a single- or multiple-position telephone switchboard handling incoming, outgoing, intraplant, or office calls. Performs full telephone information service or handles complex calls, such as conference, collect, overseas, or similar calls, either in addition to doing routine work as described for switchboard operator, class B, or as a full-time assignment. (*Full* telephone information service occurs when the establishment has varied functions that are not readily understandable for telephone information purposes, e.g., because of overlapping or interrelated functions, and consequently present frequent problems as to which extensions are appropriate for calls.)

Class B. Operates a single- or multiple-position telephone switchboard handling incoming, outgoing, intraplant, or office calls. May handle routine long distance calls and record tolls. May perform limited telephone information service. (*Limited* telephone information service occurs if the functions of the establishment serviced are readily understandable for telephone information purposes, or if the requests are routine, e.g., giving extension numbers when specific names are furnished, or if complex calls are referred to another operator.)

Switchboard Operator-Receptionist

In addition to performing duties of operator on a single-position or monitor-type switchboard, acts as receptionist and may also type or perform routine clerical work as part of regular duties. This typing or clerical work may take the major part of this worker's time while at switchboard.

Tabulating-Machine Operator

Class A. Operates a variety of tabulating or electrical accounting machines, typically including such machines as the tabulator, calculator, interpreter, collator, and others. Performs complete reporting and tabulating assignments typically involve a variety of long and complex reports which often are of irregular or nonrecurring type requiring some planning and sequencing of steps to be taken. As a more experienced operator, is typically involved in training new operators in machine operations, or partially trained operators in wiring from diagrams and operating sequences of long and complex reports. Does not include working supervisors performing tabulating-machine operations and day-to-day supervision of the work and production of a group of tabulating-maching operators.

Class B. Operates a more difficult tabulating or electrical accounting machines such as the tabulator and calculator, in addition to the sorter, reproducer, and collator. This work is performed under specific instructions and may include the performance of some wiring from diagrams. The work typically involves, for example, tabulations involving a repetitive accounting exercise, a complete but small tabulating study, or parts of a longer and more complex report. Such reports and studies are usually of a recurring nature where the procedures are well established. May also include the training of new employees in the basic operation of the machine.

Class C. Operates simple tabulating or electrical accounting machines such as the sorter, reproducing punch, collator, etc., with specific instructions. May include simple wiring from diagrams and some filing work. The work typically involves portions of a work unit, for example, individual sorting or collating runs or repetitive operations.

Transcribing-Machine Operator, General

Primary duty is to transcribe dictation involving a normal routine vocabulary from transcribing-machine records. May also type from written copy and do simple clerical work. Workers transcribing dictation involving a varied technical or specialized vocabulary such as legal briefs or reports on scientific research are not included. A worker who takes dictation in shorthand or by Stenotype or similar machine is classified as a "stenographer, general."

Typist

Uses a typewriter to make copies of various material or to make out bills after calculations have been made by another person. May include typing of stencils, mats, or similar materials for use in duplicating processes. May do clerical work involving little special training, such as keeping simple records, filing records and reports, or sorting and distributing incoming mail.

> *Class A*. Performs one or more of the following: Typing material in final form when it involves combining material from several sources or responsibility for correct spelling syllabication, punctuation, etc., of technical or unusual words or foreign language material; and planning layout and typing of complicated statistical tables to maintain uniformity and balance in spacing. May type routine form letters varying details to suit circumstances.

> *Class B*. Performs one or more of the following: Copy typing from rough or clear drafts; routine typing of forms, insurance policies, etc.; and setting up simple standard tabulations, or copying more complex tables already set up and spaced properly.

Professional and Technical Occupations

Computer Operator

Monitors and operates the control console of a digital computer to process data according to operating instructions, usually prepared by a programmer. Work includes most of the following: Studies instructions to determine equipment setup and operations; loads equipment with required items (tape reels, cards, etc.); switches necessary auxiliary equipment into circuit, and starts and operates computer; makes adjustments to computer to correct operating problems and meets special conditions; reviews errors made during operation and determines cause or refers problem to supervisor or programmer; and maintains operating records. May test and assist in correcting program.

Computer operators are classified as follows:

> *Class A*. Operates independently, or under only general direction, a computer running programs with most of the following characteristics: new programs are frequently tested and introduced; scheduling requirements are

of critical importance to minimize downtime; the programs are of complex design so that identification of error source often requires a working knowledge of the total program, and alternate programs may not be available. May give direction and guidance to lower level operators.

Programers are classified as follows:

Class A. Works independently or under only general direction on complex problems which require competence in all phases of programing concepts and practices. Working from diagrams and charts which identify the nature of desired results, major processing steps to be accomplished, and the relationships between various steps of the problem solving routine; plans the full range of programing actions needed to efficiently utilize the computer system in achieving desired end products.

At this level, programing is difficult because computer equipment must be organized to produce several interrelated but diverse products from numerous and diverse data elements. A wide variety and extensive number of internal processing actions must occur. This requires such actions as development of common operations which can be reused, establishment of linkage points between operations, adjustments to data when program requirements exceed computer storage capacity, and substantial manipulation and resequencing of data elements to form a highly integrated program.

May provide functional direction to lower-level programers who are assigned to assist.

Class B. Works independently or under only general direction on relatively simple programs, or on simple segments of complex programs. Programs (or segments) usually process information to produce data in two or three varied sequences or formats. Reports and listings are produced by refining, adapting, arraying, or making minor additions to or deletions from input data which are readily available. While numerous records may be processed, the data have been refined in prior actions so that the accuracy and sequencing of data can be tested by using a few routine checks. Typically, the program deals with routine record-keeping-type operations, or

Works on complex programs (as described for class A) under close direction of a higher level programer or supervisor. May assist higher level programer by independently performing less difficult tasks assigned, and performing more difficult tasks under fairly close direction.

May guide or instruct lower level programers.

Class C. Makes practical applications of programing practices and concepts usually learned in formal training courses. Assignments are designed to develop competence in the application of standard procedures to routine problems. Receives close supervision on new aspects of assignments; and work is reviewed to verify its accuracy and conformance with required procedures.

Computer Systems Analyst, Business

Analyzes business problems to formulate procedures for solving them by use of electronic data processing equipment. Develops a complete description of all specifications needed to enable programers to prepare required digital computer programs. Work involves most of the following: analyzes subject-matter operations to be automated and identifies conditions and criteria required to achieve satisfactory results; specifies number and types of records, files, and documents to be used; outlines actions to be performed by personnel and computers in sufficient detail for presentation to management and for programing (typically this involves preparation of work and data flow charts); coordinates the development of test problems and participates in trial runs of new and revised systems; and recommends equipment changes to obtain more effective overall operations. (Note: Workers performing both systems analysis and programing should be classified as systems analysis if this is the skill used to determine their pay).

Does not include employees primarily responsible for the management or supervision of other electronic data processing (EDP) employees, or systems analysts primarily concerned with scientific or engineering problems.

Systems analysts are classified as follow:

Class A. Works independently or under only general direction on complex problems involving all phases of systems analysis. Problems are complex because of diverse sources of input data and multiple-use requirements of output data. (For example, develops an integrated production scheduling, inventory control, cost analysis, and sales analysis record in which every item of each type is automatically processed through the full system of records and appropriate follow-up actions are initiated by the computer.) Confers with persons concerned to determine the data processing problems and advises systems of data processing operations. Makes recommendations, if needed, for approval of major systems installations or changes and for obtaining equipment.

May provide functional direction to lower level systems analysts who are assigned to assist.

Class B. Works independently or under only general direction on problems that are relatively uncomplicated to analyze, plan, program, and operate. Problems are of limited complexity because sources of input data are homogeneous and the output data are closely related. (For example, develops systems for: maintaining depositor accounts in a bank, maintaining accounts receivable in a retail establishment, or maintaining inventory accounts in a manufacturing or wholesale establishment.) Confers with persons concerned to determine the data process problems and advises subject-matter personnel on the implications of the data processing systems to be applied, or

Works on a segments of a complex data processing scheme or system, as described for class A. Works independently on routine assignments and receives instruction and guidance on complex assignments. Work is reviewed for accuracy of judgment, compliance with instructions, and to insure proper alignment with the overall system.

Class C. Works under immediate supervision, carrying out analyses as assigned, usually of a single activity. Assignments are designed to develop and expand practical experience in the application of procedures and skills required for systems analysis work. For example, may assist a higher-level systems analyst by preparing the detailed specifications required by programers from information developed by the higher level analyst.

Draftsman

Class A. Plans the graphic presentation of complex items having distinctive design features that differ significantly from established drafting precedents. Works in close support with the design originator, and may recommend minor design changes. Analyzes the effect of each change on the details of form, function, and positional relationships of components and parts. Works with a minimum of supervisory assistance. Completed work is reviewed by design originator for consistency with prior engineering determinations. May either prepare drawings, or direct their preparation by lower level draftsmen.

Class B. Performs nonroutine and complex drafting assignments that require the application of most of the standardized drawing techniques regularly used. Duties typically involve such work as: prepares working drawings of subassemblies with irregular shapes, multiple functions, and precise positional relationships between components; prepares architectural drawings for construction of a building including detail drawings of foundations, wall sections, floor plans, and roof. Uses accepted formulas and manuals in making necessary computations to determine quantities of materials to be used, load capacities, strengths, stresses, etc. Receives initial instructions, requirements, and advice from supervisor. Completed work is checked for technical adequacy.

Class C. Prepares detail drawings of single units or parts for engineering, construction, manufacturing, or repair purposes. Types of drawings prepared include isometric projections (depicting three dimensions in accurate scale) and sectional views to clarify positioning of components and convey needed information. Consolidates details from a number of sources and adjusts or transposes scale as required. Suggested methods of approach, applicable precedents, and advice on source materials are given with initial assignments. Instructions are less complete when assignments recur. Work may be spot-checked during progress.

Draftsman-Tracer

Copies plans and drawings prepared by others by placing tracing cloth or paper over drawings and tracing with pen or pencil (does not include tracing limited to plans primarily consisting of straight lines and a large scale not requiring close delineation). *and/or*

Prepares simple or repetitive drawings of easily visualized items. Work is closely supervised during progress.

Nurse, Industrial (Registered)

A registered nurse who gives nursing service under general medical direction to ill or injured employees or other persons who become ill or suffer an accident on the premises of a factory or other establishment. Duties involve a combination of the following: giving first aid to the ill or injured; attending to subsequent dressing of employees' injuries; keeping records of patients treated; preparing accident reports for compensation or other purposes; assisting in physical examinations and health evaluations of applicants and employees; and planning and carrying out programs involving health education, accident prevention, evaluation of plant environment, or other activities affecting the health, welfare, and safety of all personnel.

**Appendix B
Supplementary Tables**

Table B-1
Expected and Actual Distribution of Firms by Percent Female and City: Selected Occupations

Occupation	Percent Female												Total
	0	1-9	10-19	20-29	30-39	40-49	50-59	60-69	70-79	80-89	90-99	100	
Accounting clerk													
Class A													
Boston (P = 0.694)													
Expected	14.82	0.0	0.12	1.63	4.54	2.50	22.74	24.17	19.65	11.47	0.68	51.66	154
Actual	23.00	1.00	0.0	3.00	10.00	1.00	10.00	9.00	4.00	5.00	4.00	84.00	154
New York (P = 0.648)													
Expected	41.37	0.0	0.45	4.96	10.74	9.90	61.55	51.48	32.01	18.71	1.17	102.66	335
Actual	52.00	1.00	5.00	10.00	16.00	10.00	26.00	16.00	16.00	13.00	4.00	166.00	335
Philadelphia (P = 0.731)													
Expected	16.14	0.0	0.04	1.22	3.12	2.48	21.34	20.82	18.91	15.37	1.06	70.49	171
Actual	29.00	0.0	1.00	4.00	4.00	2.00	11.00	9.00	7.00	11.00	3.00	90.00	171
Accounting clerk													
Class B													
Boston (P = 0.925)													
Expected	3.44	0.0	0.0	0.01	0.21	0.05	3.60	3.89	4.49	19.17	17.58	109.60	162
Actual	5.00	0.0	0.0	0.0	2.00	1.00	1.00	5.00	5.00	7.00	11.00	125.00	162
New York (P = 0.759)													
Expected	19.91	0.0	0.07	2.09	5.66	2.89	33.02	40.79	51.86	39.24	6.48	120.00	322
Actual	24.00	1.00	2.00	7.00	12.00	3.00	24.00	10.00	22.00	18.00	12.00	187.00	322
Philadelphia (P = 0.883)													
Expected	5.85	0.0	0.0	0.11	0.53	0.17	8.30	6.50	10.35	24.91	9.96	103.37	170
Actual	10.00	0.0	1.00	2.00	3.00	2.00	5.00	2.00	2.00	8.00	4.00	131.00	170

Order clerk													
Boston ($P = 0.615$)													
Expected	8.73	0.0	0.23	2.49	2.61	2.41	13.72	7.56	8.36	3.01	0.09	17.79	67
Actual	13.00	0.0	4.00	0.0	0.0	0.0	4.00	0.0	1.00	3.00	0.0	42.00	67
New York ($P = 0.833$)													
Expected	4.36	0.0	0.01	0.24	0.63	0.36	7.61	6.47	12.39	18.21	4.65	51.08	106
Actual	12.00	0.0	2.00	2.00	1.00	1.00	3.00	5.00	0.0	3.00	1.00	76.00	106
Philadelphia ($P = 0.712$)													
Expected	6.20	0.0	0.03	0.40	1.98	1.01	6.69	10.23	6.46	5.37	0.20	23.43	62
Actual	10.00	1.00	1.00	0.0	3.00	0.0	1.00	2.00	1.00	0.0	0.0	43.00	62
Payroll clerk													
New York ($P = 0.855$)													
Expected	14.85	0.0	0.0	0.22	1.83	0.26	10.64	14.25	11.51	16.32	3.77	149.35	223
Actual	24.00	0.0	1.00	2.00	2.00	1.00	4.00	13.00	4.00	2.00	0.0	170.00	223
Office boy/girl													
Boston ($P = 0.327$)													
Expected	33.70	0.24	3.87	12.30	13.40	5.71	12.62	3.86	1.12	0.24	0.0	11.93	99
Actual	56.00	1.00	3.00	2.00	3.00	1.00	4.00	2.00	2.00	3.00	2.00	20.00	99
New York ($P = 0.248$)													
Expected	107.99	2.66	23.31	50.21	33.71	10.72	19.68	6.98	1.08	0.30	0.0	22.36	279
Actual	184.00	5.00	9.00	13.00	6.00	2.00	7.00	7.00	4.00	2.00	5.00	35.00	279
Philadelphia ($P = 0.400$)													
Expected	37.78	0.03	2.19	10.45	14.74	9.11	20.64	9.18	2.28	1.03	0.0	20.57	128
Actual	71.00	0.0	1.00	5.00	6.00	3.00	5.00	3.00	3.00	3.00	2.00	26.00	128
Tabulating-machine operator Class A													
New York ($P = 0.380$)													
Expected	15.02	0.05	1.25	4.45	6.14	4.56	10.23	2.34	0.38	0.33	0.0	7.27	52
Actual	36.00	1.00	1.00	0.0	1.00	0.0	0.0	1.00	0.0	0.0	1.00	11.00	52

Table B-1 (cont.)

Occupation	Percent Female												Total
	0	1-9	10-19	20-29	30-39	40-49	50-59	60-69	70-79	80-89	90-99	100	
Class B													
New York (P = 0.271)													
Expected	25.38	0.39	3.44	11.07	8.62	2.44	6.51	1.56	0.32	0.07	0.0	6.20	66
Actual	45.00	2.00	3.00	2.00	1.00	3.00	2.00	0.0	1.00	0.0	0.0	7.00	66
Professional and Technical													
Systems Analyst													
Class B													
New York (P = 0.149)													
Expected	48.53	3.37	14.36	10.02	6.18	0.73	5.30	0.84	0.12	0.01	0.0	3.53	93
Actual	66.00	2.00	4.00	7.00	4.00	3.00	5.00	1.00	0.0	0.0	0.0	1.00	93
Computer Programer													
Class A													
New York (P = 0.208)													
Expected	62.36	0.71	9.78	15.95	8.21	3.19	9.73	1.69	0.25	0.08	0.0	10.05	122
Actual	82.00	1.00	8.00	6.00	7.00	2.00	5.00	3.00	1.00	1.00	0.0	6.00	122
Class B													
Boston (P = 0.411)													
Expected	20.37	0.03	1.10	7.48	6.63	7.82	12.96	4.65	1.97	0.86	0.01	12.12	76
Actual	38.00	0.0	4.00	8.00	3.00	3.00	9.00	3.00	1.00	0.0	0.0	7.00	76
New York (P = 0.261)													
Expected	62.16	0.81	7.93	15.29	13.93	3.99	16.20	2.79	0.46	0.10	0.0	14.35	138
Actual	84.00	0.0	8.00	6.00	11.00	5.00	8.00	4.00	2.00	0.0	0.0	10.00	138

Philadelphia (P = 0.184)													
Expected	42.28	2.49	7.63	10.60	5.48	2.48	5.88	1.18	0.06	0.05	0.0	4.86	83
Actual	53.00	0.0	4.00	4.00	6.00	2.00	4.00	5.00	1.00	0.0	0.0	4.00	83
Class C													
New York (P = 0.309)													
Expected	34.22	0.28	3.71	7.27	9.23	4.08	10.80	2.61	0.26	0.23	0.0	11.33	84
Actual	50.00	0.0	2.00	4.00	3.00	4.00	14.00	2.00	0.0	0.0	0.0	5.00	84
Computer operator													
Class B													
New York (P = 0.101)													
Expected	108.06	12.11	14.80	10.21	5.91	0.78	7.47	0.66	0.05	0.0	0.0	4.95	165
Actual	136.00	4.00	3.00	4.00	3.00	0.0	3.00	2.00	0.0	0.0	0.0	10.00	165
Philadelphia (P = 0.103)													
Expected	71.30	5.74	11.21	7.71	5.03	0.41	5.39	0.52	0.04	0.0	0.0	2.66	110
Actual	89.00	2.00	3.00	2.00	2.00	0.0	4.00	1.00	0.0	0.0	0.0	7.00	110

Source: Computed from unpublished Bureau of Labor Statistics data collected for the *Area Wage Surveys* between April and November 1970.

Note: If p_i is the percentage that women comprise of total employment within the occupational category in establishment i, then the twelve sex composition categories above are defined as $p_i = 0, 0 < p_i < 10, 10 \leqslant p_i < 20, 20 \leqslant p_i < 30, \ldots, 90 \leqslant p_i < 100, p_i = 100$.

Table B-2
Distribution of Sample Establishments by Industry, Union Status, and Size of Firm: Boston, New York, and Philadelphia

Industry	Total	U_0	U_1	U_2	S_0	S_1
Boston	248	149	18	81	197	51
Manufacturing	77	30	5	42	59	18
20. Food and kindred products	10	1	1	8	8	2
35. Machinery, except electrical	10	5	0	5	7	3
36. Electrical and electronic machinery, equipment, and supplies	15	9	1	5	9	6
Other nondurable goods	26	7	3	16	21	5
22. Textile mill products	2	0	0	2	2	0
23. Apparel and other finished fabric products	3	1	0	2	3	0
26. Paper and allied products	2	0	0	2	2	0
27. Printing, publishing, and allied industries	8	2	3	3	5	3
30. Rubber and miscellaneous plastics products	7	3	0	4	6	1
31. Leather and leather products	4	1	0	3	3	1
Other durable goods, including chemicals	16	8	0	8	14	2
28. Chemicals and allied products	2	2	0	0	2	0
32. Stone, clay, glass, and concrete products	1	1	0	0	1	0
34. Fabricated metal products	4	0	0	4	4	0
38. Instruments and related products	6	3	0	3	5	1
39. Miscellaneous manufacturing	3	2	0	1	2	1
Transportation and public utilities	14	0	8	6	10	4
41. Local and suburban transit; interurban highway	1	0	0	1	1	0
42. Motor freight transportation and warehousing	5	0	2	3	5	0
45. Air transportation	3	0	1	2	0	3
48. Communication	1	0	1	0	1	0
49. Electric, gas and sanitary services	4	0	4	0	3	1

Wholesale trade

50. Wholesale trade-durable goods	42	26	2	14	41	1
Retail trade	30	21	3	6	17	13
53. General merchandise stores	12	8	3	1	6	6
Other retail	18	13	0	5	11	7
52. Building materials, hardware, garden supply, mobile home dealers	1	1	0	0	1	0
54. Food stores	7	3	0	4	2	5
55. Automotive dealers; gasoline service stations	1	1	0	0	1	0
56. Apparel and accessory stores	2	2	0	0	2	0
57. Furniture, home furnishings and equipment stores	2	1	0	1	2	0
58. Eating and drinking places	5	5	0	0	3	2
Finance and insurance	36	36	0	0	26	10
Finance	15	15	0	0	11	4
60. Banking	11	11	0	0	7	4
62. Security and commodity brokers, dealers, exchanges, services	4	4	0	0	4	0
Insurance	21	21	0	0	15	6
63. Insurance	19	19	0	0	13	6
64. Insurance agents, brokers, and services	2	2	0	0	2	0
Services	49	36	0	13	44	5
Personal services	10	3	0	7	9	1
70. Hotels and other lodging places	8	2	0	6	7	1
72. Personal services	2	1	0	1	2	0
Business and repair services	29	23	0	6	25	4
73. Business services	27	22	0	5	23	4
75. Automotive repair, services, and garages	2	1	0	1	2	0
89. Miscellaneous services	10	10	0	0	10	0

132

Table B-2 (cont.)

Industry	Total	U_0	U_1	U_2	S_0	S_1
New York	572	266	83	223	410	162
Manufacturing	192	58	23	111	148	44
20. Food and kindred products	24	3	3	18	18	6
23. Apparel and other finished fabric products	14	0	2	12	13	1
27. Printing, publishing, and allied industries	25	13	6	6	17	8
28. Chemicals and allied products	16	10	1	5	10	6
35. Machinery, except electrical	10	5	2	3	5	5
36. Electrical and electronic machinery, equipment, and supplies	27	8	3	16	23	4
38. Instruments and related products	11	2	2	7	6	5
39. Miscellaneous manufacturing	14	2	2	10	13	1
Other nondurable goods	19	5	1	13	16	3
22. Textile mill products	4	3	0	1	2	2
26. Paper and allied products	8	2	0	6	7	1
30. Rubber and miscellaneous plastics products	3	0	1	2	3	0
31. Leather and leather products	4	0	0	4	4	0
Other durable goods, including petroleum	32	10	1	21	27	5
19. Ordinance and accessories	2	0	0	2	2	0
25. Furniture and fixtures	3	1	0	2	3	0
29. Petroleum refining and related industries	3	3	0	0	2	1
32. Stone, clay, glass, and concrete products	3	0	0	3	2	1
33. Primary metal industries	7	2	0	5	7	0
34. Fabricated metal products	7	2	1	4	6	1
37. Transportation equipment	7	2	0	5	5	2
Transportation and public utilities	57	13	16	28	27	30
44. Water transportation	11	6	3	2	5	6
45. Air transportation	15	1	3	11	7	8
48. Communication	13	1	6	6	1	12

Other transportation and public utilities	18	5	4	9	14	4
40. Railroad transportation	2	1	0	1	1	1
41. Local and suburban transit; interurban highway passenger transportation	1	0	0	1	1	0
42. Motor freight transportation and warehousing	7	1	1	5	7	0
47. Transportation services	4	2	0	2	4	0
49. Electric, gas and sanitary services	4	1	3	0	1	3
Wholesale trade						
50. Wholesale trade-durable goods	87	42	12	33	84	3
Retail trade	75	32	20	23	34	41
53. General merchandise stores	33	22	11	0	6	27
56. Apparel and accessory stores	16	5	7	4	12	4
Other retail	26	5	2	19	16	10
52. Building materials, hardware, garden supply, mobile home dealers	1	0	0	1	1	0
54. Food stores	8	0	0	8	3	5
57. Furniture, home furnishings and equipment stores	2	0	1	1	2	0
58. Eating and drinking places	11	4	0	7	6	5
59. Miscellaneous retail	4	1	1	2	4	0
Finance, insurance, and real estate	76	69	0	7	52	24
Banking and credit	24	24	0	0	14	10
60. Banking	21	21	0	0	11	10
61. Other credit agencies	3	3	0	0	3	0
Brokers and investment offices	23	23	0	0	15	8
62. Security and commodity brokers, dealers, exchanges, services	20	20	0	0	13	7
67. Holding and other investment offices	3	3	0	0	2	1

Table B-2 (cont.)

Industry	Total	U_0	U_1	U_2	S_0	S_1
Insurance	22	21	0	1	16	6
63. Insurance	19	18	0	1	14	5
64. Insurance agents, brokers, and service	3	3	0	0	2	1
65. Real estate	7	1	0	6	7	0
Services	85	52	12	21	65	20
Personal services	21	1	9	11	16	5
70. Hotels and other lodging places	14	0	4	10	11	3
72. Personal services	7	1	5	1	5	2
Business and repair services	41	33	2	6	30	11
73. Busines services	40	33	2	5	29	11
75. Automotive repair, services, and garages	1	0	0	1	1	0
Other services	23	18	1	4	19	4
78. Motion pictures	5	1	1	3	5	0
86. Membership organizations	2	1	0	1	2	0
89. Miscellaneous services	16	16	0	0	12	4
Philadelphia	386	133	54	149	239	97
Manufacturing	168	34	40	94	106	62
20. Food and kindred products	19	1	1	17	13	6
23. Apparel and other finished fabric products	11	4	7	0	10	1
27. Printing, publishing, and allied industries	10	2	0	8	4	6
28. Chemicals and allied products	16	5	3	8	8	8
33. Primary metal industries	13	4	9	0	6	7
34. Fabricated metal products	13	1	1	11	9	4
35. Machinery, except electrical	18	4	3	11	11	7
36. Electrical and electronic machinery, equipment and supplies	19	2	5	12	10	9

Other nondurable goods	19	3	3	13	16	3
22. Textile mill products	7	1	0	6	7	0
26. Paper and allied products	7	1	0	6	5	2
30. Rubber and miscellaneous plastics products	4	1	3	0	3	1
31. Leather and leather products	1	0	0	1	1	0
Other durable goods, including petroleum	30	8	8	14	19	11
19. Ordinance and accessories	3	3	0	0	2	1
25. Furniture and fixtures	2	0	0	2	2	0
29. Petroleum refining and related industries	5	1	4	0	1	4
32. Stone, clay, glass, and concrete products	5	1	0	4	5	0
37. Transportation equipment	7	0	3	4	3	4
38. Instruments and related products	6	3	1	2	4	2
39. Miscellaneous manufacturing	2	0	0	2	2	0
Transportation and public utilities	21	4	6	11	20	1
40. Railroad transportation	1	0	1	0	1	0
42. Motor freight transportation and warehousing	9	0	2	7	9	0
44. Water transportation	2	2	0	0	2	0
45. Air transportation	3	1	0	2	3	0
46. Pipe lines, except natural gas	1	0	1	0	1	0
48. Communication	5	1	2	2	4	1
Wholesale trade						
50. Wholesale trade-durable goods	39	13	3	23	37	2
Retail trade	27	17	3	7	8	19
53. General merchandise stores	14	11	3	0	2	12
Other retail	13	6	0	7	6	7
54. Food stores	6	2	0	4	2	4
56. Apparel and accessory stores	1	1	0	0	1	0
58. Eating and drinking places	4	1	0	3	1	3
59. Miscellaneous retail	2	2	0	0	2	0

Table B-2 (cont.)

Industry	Total	U_0	U_1	U_2	S_0	S_1
Finance, insurance, and real estate	39	39	0	0	28	11
Finance	15	15	0	0	9	6
60. Banking	12	12	0	0	6	6
61. Other credit agencies	1	1	0	0	1	0
62. Security and commodity brokers, dealers, exchanges, services	2	2	0	0	2	0
Insurance and real estate	24	24	0	0	19	5
63. Insurance	20	20	0	0	15	5
64. Insurance agents, brokers and service	3	3	0	0	3	0
65. Real estate	1	1	0	0	1	0
Services	42	26	2	14	40	2
Personal services	13	1	2	10	13	0
70. Hotels and other lodging places	7	1	0	6	7	0
72. Personal services	6	0	2	4	6	0
Business and repair services	19	15	0	4	17	2
73. Business services	18	15	0	3	16	2
75. Automotive repair, services and garages	1	0	0	1	1	0
Other services	10	10	0	0	10	0
86. Membership organizations	1	1	0	0	1	0
89. Miscellaneous services	9	9	0	0	9	0

Notes

Notes

Chapter 1
Introduction

1. See, for example, such economy-wide studies as Sanborn (1964); Fuchs (1971); Oaxaca (1973); and Sawhill (1973). For a critique of the narrow focus of such studies, see Madden (1973, pp. 20-21).

2. For a study of intraoccupational pay differentials utilizing data on individuals, see Hamilton (1973). For studies of intraoccupational pay differences employing aggregate establishment data, see McNulty (1967) and Buckley (1971).

3. For examples of the historical antecedents of this approach, see Fawcett (1918); Webb (1919); and Edgeworth (1922). For examples of current theoretical and empirical support for this view, see Bergmann (1974); Fuchs (1971); Blau (Weisskoff) (1972); Zellner (1972); Sawhill (1973); and Blau and Jusenius (1976).

4. Computed from *U.S. Census of the Population* (1973), table 221. See following discussion in the text for a more detailed consideration of these differences.

5. For empirical studies of interoccupational segregation see Oppenheimer (1970) and Gross (1968).

6. For examples of application of the Index, see Gross (1968) and Tauber and Tauber (1965). For a discussion of the mathematical properties and interrelationships of alternative measures of segregation, see Duncan and Duncan (1955).

7. The source for the 1950 and 1960 figures is Gross (1968), table 2. The 1970 figure was computed from *U.S. Census of the Population* (1973), table 221.

Chapter 2
The Constraints

1. See, for example, Doeringer and Piore (1971); Dunlop (1957); Livernash (1957); and Kerr (1954).

2. For a fuller treatment of the implications of these considerations within the context of the internal labor market, see Doeringer and Piore (1971), pp. 74-78. In addition to the direct costs of turnover, employers may be concerned with the adverse effect of losses of employees on the firm's reputation and with the uncertain quality of new applicants. See Lester (1954, pp. 29-31).

139

3. See Kerr (1954, pp. 103-106), and Doeringer and Piore (1971, p. 75). For evidence of the inverse relationship between job separations and seniority, see Organization for Economic Co-operation and Development (1965), pp. 67-68, and Reynolds (1951), pp. 21-22. Reynolds points out that risk aversion may be an element in the reluctance of workers to change employers. Particularly in unionized plants, seniority offers some protection against layoffs. In addition, "a new job cannot be 'sized up' accurately until you have worked on it for a while. If you give up your present job and the new job does not turn out as expected, you have made a serious and irretrievable error."

4. For descriptions of job evaluation techniques and methods of performance appraisal see, for example, Pigors and Meyers (1969, pp. 345-70), and Flippo (1971, pp. 227-92).

5. See also Piore (1973). For evidence of the negative effect of a compression of the wage structure on employee morale and turnover in clerical occupations, see Schultz (1962, pp. 128-29).

6. For discussions of these and other issues relating to the functions and efficiency of the internal wage structure, see Doeringer and Piore (1971, ch. 4), and Wachter (1974, pp. 644-48).

7. See, for example, Lester (1954, pp. 73-87); Rees and Schultz (1970, pp. 36-54); and Reynolds (1951, pp. 155-203). For an econometric analysis of establishment wage dispersion in the Boston labor market, see Wachter (1970, pp. 167-223).

8. See, for example, Piore (1971), and Gordon (1972).

9. For evidence of the inverse relationship between labor turnover and earnings levels, see Organization for Economic Co-operation and Development (1965, pp. 52-54). A recent study by Deutsch, Shea, and Evans, recruitment advertising specialists, of female white-collar personnel who had recently changed jobs indicates that these factors are of considerable importance in explaining turnover among women clerical workers. The principal reasons given for leaving the employer were lack of interesting work, salary dissatisfaction, and the lack of prospects for added responsibility (1971, pp. 565-56). Poor supervision, job dissatisfaction and poor working conditions also contribute to employee absenteeism. See Hartman (1971).

10. Reynolds argues that the high-wage firm can demand superior performance because workers who know that they have a job that pays above the area level will want to keep it. See Reynolds (1974, p. 201). For an approach to employee motivation, see Herzberg (1968). For case studies of the impact of one motivational technique—job enrichment—on employee turnover, attitudes, and productivity, see Maher (1971).

11. See Lester (1954, pp. 57-58), and Hildebrand (1963, pp. 277-78).

12. The direct evidence from local labor-market studies on this point is somewhat contradictory. That is, while some employers claim that the wage

position of the firm relative to other establishments strongly affects the quality of applicants, others deny a relationship. It may be that firms have over time adjusted their hiring standards to their position in the wage hierarchy and thus find no difficulty meeting them, unless their wage position relative to other firms deteriorates. See, for example, Lester (1954, pp. 47-51); Rees and Schultz (1970, pp. 50-52); and Schultz (1962, pp. 124-33).

13. See, for example, Masters (1969); Weiss (1966); Lewis (1963); Fuchs (1968); and Segal (1964).

14. See Masters (1969), and Lester (1967). Lester points out that even if firm size is taken as a proxy for market power, it is not clear whether we should expect it to be positively related to wage rates (due to monopolistic or oligopolistic power in the product market) or negatively related to wage rates (due to monopsonistic or oligopsonistic power in the labor market).

15. A considerable number of the studies of this question are concerned with interfirm and interindustry variations in pay rates among production workers, and thus are suggestive, but not conclusive, for our sample of white-collar occupations. We focus our discussion on studies that have included office workers. For studies dealing with production workers see, for example, Raimon (1953); Slichter (1950); and Wachtel and Betsey (1972).

Chapter 3
The Model

1. It is necessary to refer to related occupations because not all occupations are equally closely tied by technology, administrative arrangements (e.g., promotion ladders), and customary factors. Related occupations, termed *job clusters*, are more likely to have a similar wage ranking in the local labor market. See Dunlop (1957, pp. 129-30), and Livernash (1957, pp. 148-60). The determination of broad job clusters is to some extent an empirical question. It is assumed that the office jobs in our sample comprise such a group.

2. This model is somewhat similar to Thurow's "job competition" model (1975).

3. It is important to note that detailed job classifications may not be considered complete guarantees of similar work. The consistency with which they are applied is also an important factor. In this respect it appears to us that the role of the Bureau of Labor Statistics field staff is particularly important. The field staff is regionally based, and since panel data are employed in the collection of data for the Area Wage Surveys, Bureau of Labor Statistics representatives have the opportunity to become familiar, over a period of time, with the participating firms in their area. Moreover, since they determine the classification of workers into occupation-skill class categories, greater consis-

tency may be expected than is the case when, for example, reliance is placed on employer or employee self-reporting. For a discussion of the inconsistencies and other problems in self-reporting, see James G. Scoville (1972, pp. 98-111).

4. An additional consideration worth noting is that we have no data on fringe benefits. Were the magnitude of fringe benefits negatively related to wage rates, this might act to offset interfirm variation in wages. In fact, the available evidence indicates quite the contrary, namely, that the level of fringe benefits is positively correlated with wage rates and thus would not help to explain the variation in wage rates. See, for example, Reynolds (1951, pp. 220-22), and Rees and Schultz (1970, pp. 77-79).

Chapter 4
Occupational Wage Rates and Employment Patterns

1. See, for example, Piore (1971), and Lester (1954, ch. 3). See chapter 2 of this book for a fuller development of these points and related issues.

Chapter 5
Establishment Wage Rates and the Sex Composition of Employment

1. For discussions of the importance of this factor, see Rees and Schultz (1970, pp. 36-44), and Wachter (1970, pp. 190-94).

2. See Hammermesh (1971, pp. 161-62); Raimon and Stoikov (1969); and Rees and Schultz (1970, pp. 181-84). The union variable employed by Rees and Schultz for white-collar workers was "union in the establishment." This is roughly the same as our "plant-only" variable, since white-collar workers were unionized in only a few of the establishments in their sample.

Chapter 6
Conclusions and Recommendations

1. For an elucidation and comparison of demand- and supply-side explanations, see Blau and Jusenius (1976).

2. The major cases include *Weeks* v. *Southern Bell Telephone*, 408 F. 2d 228 (5th Cir. 1969), *reversing in pertinent part*, 277 F. Supp. 117 (S.D. Ga. 1967); *Rosenfeld* v. *Southern Pacific Co.*, 444 F. 2d 1219 (9th Cir. 1971); and *Dias* v. *Pan American World Airways, Inc.*, 444 F. 2d 385 (5th Cir.), *cert. denied*, 404 U.S. 950 (1971).

3. *Phillips* v. *Martin Marietta Corp.*, 400 U.S. 542 (1971).

Appendix A
Occupational Descriptions

1. U.S. Department of Labor (1970, pp. 78-81). Since these descriptions have for the most part been taken verbatim from this source with only small changes in style and punctuation, quotation marks have been omitted.

References

References

Books

Becker, Gary S. *The Economics of Discrimination.* Chicago: University of Chicago Press, 1957.

Bluestone, Barry, Murphy, William M., and Stevenson, Mary. *Low Wages and the Working Poor: Policy Papers in Human Resources and Industrial Relations,* vol. 22. Ann Arbor: Institute of Labor and Industrial Relations, University of Michigan, Wayne State University, July 1973.

Doeringer, Peter B. and Piore, Michael J. *Internal Labor Markets and Manpower Analysis.* Lexington, Mass.: D.C. Heath, 1971.

Exploitation from 9 to 5. Report of the Twentieth Century Fund Task Force on Women and Employment. Lexington, Mass.: Lexington Books, D.C. Heath and Company, 1975. Background Paper by Adele Simmons, Ann Freedman, Margaret Dunkle, and Francine Blau.

Flippo, Edwin B. *Principles of Personnel Management,* 3rd ed. New York: McGraw-Hill, 1971.

Fuchs, Victor R. *The Service Economy.* New York: National Bureau of Economic Research, 1968.

Gordon, David M. *Theories of Poverty and Underemployment: Orthodox, Radical, and Dual Labor Market Perspectives.* Lexington, Mass.: D.C. Heath, 1972.

Kmenta, Jan. *Elements of Econometrics.* New York: Macmillan, 1971.

Lester, Richard A. *Hiring Practices and Labor Competition.* Princeton: Industrial Relations Section, Princeton University, 1954.

Lewis, H. Gregg. *Unionism and Relative Wages in the United States: An Empirical Inquiry.* Chicago: University of Chicago Press, 1963.

Madden, Janice Fanning. *The Economics of Sex Discrimination.* Lexington, Mass.: Lexington Books, 1973.

Maher, John R., ed. *New Perspectives in Job Enrichment.* New York: Van Nostrand Reinhold, 1971.

Oppenheimer, Valerie Kincade. *The Female Labor Force in the United States: Demographic Factors Governing its Growth and Changing Composition.* Berkeley: Institute of International Studies, University of California, 1970.

Organization for Economic Cooperation and Development. *Wages and Labour Mobility.* Paris: Organization for Economic Cooperation and Development, July 1965.

Pigors, Paul and Meyers, Charles A. *Personnel Administration: A Point of View and a Method,* 6th ed. New York: McGraw-Hill.

Rees, Albert and Schultz, George P. *Workers and Wages in an Urban Labor Market.* Chicago: University of Chicago Press, 1970.

Reynolds, Lloyd G. *The Structure of Labor Markets: Wages and Labor Mobility in Theory and Practice.* New York: Harper and Brothers, 1951.

_____. *Labor Economics and Labor Relations,* 6th ed. Englewood Cliffs, N.J.: Prentice-Hall, 1974.

Scoville, James G. *Manpower and Occupational Analysis: Concepts and Measurements.* Lexington, Mass.: Lexington Books, 1972.

Slichter, Sumner H. *What's Ahead for American Business.* Boston: Little, Brown & Co., 1951.

Smith, Georgina M. *Help Wanted—Female: A Study of Demand and Supply in a Local Job Market for Women.* New Brunswick: Institute of Management and Labor Relations, Rutgers—The State University, undated.

Tauber, Karl E. and Tauber, Alma F. *Negroes in Cities: Residential Segregation and Neighborhood Change.* Chicago: Aldine, 1965.

Thurow, Lester C. *Generating Inequality: Mechanisms of Distribution in the U.S. Economy.* New York: Basic Books, 1975.

Webb, Beatrice. *The Wages of Men and Women: Should They be Equal?* London: George and Allen Unwin, 1919.

Journal Articles

Ashenfelter, Orley and Johnson, George E. "Unionism, Relative Wages, and Labor Quality in U.S. Manufacturing Industries." *International Economic Review* 13 (1972), pp. 488-509.

Bergmann, Barbara R., "Occupational Segregation, Wages and Profits when Employers Discriminate by Race or Sex." *Eastern Economic Journal* 1 (1974), pp. 103-10.

Blau (Weiskoff), Francine. ' 'Women's Place' in the Labor Market." *American Economic Review* 62 (1972), pp. 161-66.

Blau, Francine D. and Jusenius, Carol L. "Economists' Approaches to Sex Segregation in the Labor Market: An Appraisal." *Signs* 1 (1976), pp. 181-200.

Buckley, John E. 'Pay Differences Between Men and Women in the Same Job." *Monthly Labor Review* 94 (1971), pp. 36-39.

Conant, Eaton H. "Worker Efficiency and Wage Differentials in a Clerical Labor Market." *Industrial and Labor Relations Review* 16 (1963), pp. 428-33.

Dean, Burton V. "Job Evaluation Upholds Discrimination Suit." *Industrial Engineering* 3 (1971), pp. 28-31.

Deutsch, Shea, and Evans. "As You Were Saying—How to Hire a Secretary." *Personnel Journal* 50 (1971), pp. 565-66.

Duncan, Otis Dudley and Duncan, Beverly. "A Methodological Analysis of Segregation Indexes." *American Sociological Review* 20 (1955), pp. 210-17.

"EEOC Under Fire," *The Spokeswoman* 6 (1976), pp. 5-6.

Edgeworth, F.Y. "Equal Pay to Men and Women." *Economic Journal* 32 (1922), pp. 431-57.

Edwards, Harry T. "Arbitration of Employment Discrimination Cases: A Proposal for Employer and Union Representatives." *Labor Law Journal* 27 (1976), pp. 265-77.

Fawcett, Millicent G. "Equal Pay for Equal Work." *Economic Journal* 28 (1918), pp. 1-6.

Fuchs, Victor R. "Differences in Hourly Earnings Between Men and Women." *Monthly Labor Review* 94 (1971), pp. 9-15.

Gross, Edward. "Plus ça Change . . . ? The Sexual Structure of Occupations Over Time." *Social Problems* 16 (1968), pp. 198-208.

Hamilton, Mary Townsend, "Sex and Income Inequality Among the Employed." *The Annals of the American Academy of Political and Social Sciences* 409 (1973), pp. 42-52.

Hammerman, Herbert and Rogoff, Marvin. "Unions and Title VII of the Civil Rights Act of 1964." *Monthly Labor Review* 99 (1976), pp. 34-37.

Hammermesh, Daniel S. "White-Collar Unions, Blue-Collar Unions, and Wages in Manufacturing," *Industrial and Labor Relations Review* 24 (1971), pp. 159-70.

Hartman, Richard I. and Gibson, John J. "The Persistent Problem of Employee Absenteeism." *Personnel Journal* 50 (1971), pp. 535-39.

Hedges, Janice N. "Women Workers and Manpower Demands in the 1970's." *Monthly Labor Review* 93 (1970), pp. 19-29.

Herzberg, Frederick. "One More Time: How Do You Motivate Employees?" *Harvard Business Review* 46 (1968), pp. 53-62.

"In Case You Thought You Could Count on the EEOC . . . " *The Spokeswoman* 7 (1976), pp. 5-7.

Kitagawa, Evelyn M. "Components of a Difference Between Two Rates." *The Journal of the American Statistical Association* 50 (1955), pp. 1168-93.

"Labor Moves to Gut Enforcement Rules," *The Spokeswoman* 7 (1976), pp. 1-3.

Lester, Richard. "Pay Differentials by Size of Establishment." *Industrial Relations* 7 (1967), pp. 57-67.

Masters, Stanley H. "Wages and Plant Size: An Interindustry Analysis." *Review of Economics and Statistics* 51 (1969), pp. 341-45.

McNulty, Donald J. "Differences in Pay Between Men and Women Workers." *Monthly Labor Review* 90 (1967), pp. 40-43.

Mincer, Jacob and Polachek, Solomon. "Family Investments in Human Capital: Earnings of Women." *Journal of Political Economy* 82 (1974), S 76-S 108.

Piore, Michael J. "Fragments of a 'Sociological' Theory of Wages." *Industrial Relations Research Association Series: Proceedings of the Twenty-Fifth Anniversay Meetings.* Toronto, 1973.

Raimon, Robert L. and Stoikov, Vladimir. "The Effect of Blue-Collar Unionism on White-Collar Earnings." *Industrial and Labor Relations Review* 22 (1969), pp. 358-74.

Sanborn, Henry. "Pay Differences Between Men and Women." *Industrial and Labor Relations Review* 17 (1964), pp. 532-50.

Sawhill, Isabel V. "The Economics of Discrimination Against Women: Some New Findings." *Journal of Human Resources* 8 (1973), pp. 383-95.

Segal, Martin. "The Relationship Between Union Wage Impact and Market Structure." *Quarterly Journal of Economics* 78 (1964), pp. 96-114.

Slichter, Sumner H. "Notes on the Structure of Wages." *Review of Economics and Statistics* 32 (1950), pp. 80-92.

Ullman, Joseph C. "Interfirm Differences in the Cost of Search for Clerical Workers." *The Journal of Business* 41 (1968), pp. 153-65.

Wachtel, Howard M. and Betsey, Charles. "Employment at Low Wages." *Review of Economics and Statistics* 54 (1972), pp. 121-29.

Wachter, Michael L. "Cyclical Variation in the Interindustry Wage Structure." *American Economic Review* 60 (1970), pp. 75-84.

Weiss, Leonard W. "Concentration and Labor Earnings." *American Economic Review* 56 (1966), pp. 96-117.

Zellner, Harriet. "Discrimination Against Women, Occupational Segregation and the Relative Wage." *American Economic Review* 62 (1972), pp. 157-60.

Unpublished Material

Wachter, Michael L. Relative Wage Determination Among Industries: Some Theoretical and Empirical Results. Ph.D. dissertation, Harvard University, 1970.

Government Documents

Economic Report of the President, 1973. Washington, D.C.: Government Printing Office, 1973.

Equal Employment Opportunity Commission. "A Unique Competence: A Study of Equal Employment Opportunity in the Bell System." *Congressional Record: Extensions of Remarks* (February 17, 1972), 92d. Cong., 2d sess., 1972, 118, 1243-72.

U.S. Commission on Civil Rights. *The Federal Civil Rights Enforcement Effort—1974,* vol. 5, *To Eliminate Employment Discrimination.* Washington, D.C.: Government Printing Office, 1975.

U.S. Department of Commerce, Bureau of the Census. *U.S. Census of the Population, 1970, Detailed Characteristics.* Final Report PC(1)-D1, U.S. Summary. Washington, D.C.: U.S. Government Printing Office, 1973.

151

U.S. Department of Labor, Bureau of Labor Statistics. *Occupational Outlook Handbook*, 1970-71 ed. Washington, D.C.: Government Printing Office.

Essays in Collections

Arrow, Kenneth. "The Theory of Discrimination." *Discrimination in Labor Markets.* Ed. Orley Ashenfelter and Albert Rees. Princeton, New Jersey: Princeton University Press, 1973.

Bergmann, Barbara R. "Reducing the Pervasiveness of Discrimination." *Jobs for Americans.* Ed. Eli Ginzberg. Englewood Cliffs, N.J.: Prentice-Hall, 1976.

Dunlop, John T. "The Task of Contemporary Wage Theory." *New Concepts in Wage Determination.* Ed. George W. Taylor and Frank C. Pierson. New York: McGraw-Hill, 1957.

Hildebrand, George H. "External Influence and the Determination of the Internal Wage Structure." *Internal Wage Structure.* Ed. J.L. Meij. Amsterdam: North Holland, 1963.

Kassalow, Everett M. "White-Collar Unionism in the United States." *White Collar Trade Unions: Contemporary Developments in Industrial Societies.* Ed. Adoph Sturmthal. Urbana: University of Illinois Press, 1967.

Kerr, Clark. "The Balkanization of Labor Markets." *Labor Mobility and Economic Opportunity.* Cambridge, Mass.: M.I.T. Press, 1954.

Livernash, E. Robert. "The Internal Wage Structure." *New Concepts in Wage Determination.* Ed. George N. Taylor and Frank C. Pierson. New York: McGraw-Hill, 1957.

Oaxaca, Ronald. "Sex Discrimination in Wages." *Discrimination in Labor Markets.* Ed. Orley Ashenfelter and Albert Rees. Princeton, N.J.: Princeton University Press, 1973.

Piore, Michael J. "The Dual Labor Market: Theory and Implications." *Problems in Political Economy: An Urban Perspective.* Ed. David M. Gordon. Lexington, Mass.: D.C. Heath, 1971.

Schultz, George P. "A Nonunion Market for White Collar Labor." *Aspects of Labor Economics.* National Bureau of Economic Research. Princeton, N.J.: Princeton University Press, 1962.

Wachter, Michael L. "Primary and Secondary Labor Markets: A Critique of the Dual Approach." *Brookings Papers on Economic Activity*, vol. 3. Ed. Arthur M. Okun and George L. Perry. Washington, D.C.: The Brookings Institution, 1974.

Wallace, Phyllis A. "Impact of Equal Employment Opportunity Laws." *Women and the American Economy.* Ed. Juanita M. Kreps. Englewood Cliffs, N.J.: Prentice-Hall, 1976.

Index

Absenteeism, and hiring practices, 30, 34

Accountants, pay differentials among, 46

Accounting clerks, average wages for, 61, 62; distribution of women employed as, 52-54, 126; index of segregation for, 58; job description for, 114; pay differentials among, 70

Age, and hiring practices, 30

Agriculture, male-female employment in, 13, 17

Anti-discrimination policies, planning for, 104. *See also* Discrimination; Segregation

Area Wage Surveys, 4, 52

Arrow, K., 42

Ashenfelter, O., 31, 85

Barbers, representation of women among, 11

Beauticians, representation of women among, 11

Becker, G.S., 1, 21, 31, 35, 37, 40, 41, 42

Bergmann, B. 28, 103

Betsey, C., 33

Bill collectors, representation of women among, 17

Biller, machine, job description for, 113

Bluestone, B., 33

Bookkeeping-machine operator, job description for, 113-114

Boston, average wages in, 62-65; distribution of firms by percent female in, 126-129; distribution of sample establishments in, 130-131; establishment size and wage index in, 94; index of segregation for, 58; labor studies in, 52-54; pay differentials in, 79; proportion-female

index for, 88-89; representation of women in firms of, 81, 86, 87; wage standing of establishments in, 80

Bureau of Labor Statistics, 4, 52; occupational descriptions of, 113-124

Capital, human, 39

Capital-to-labor ratio, 28

Cashier, proportion of women in occupation, 18

Chicago, labor market studies in, 33

Child care, 110

Children, and hiring practices, 106

Chi-square analysis, 49; of employment patterns, 55-56

Civil Rights Act, Title VII of, 105

Clerical jobs, female concentration in, 17. *See also* Accounting clerks; Order clerks; Payroll clerks

Commission on Civil Rights, U.S., 106, 107, 108

Competition, and full employment, 110-111; among higher-level workers, 28; in industry, 41

Complaints, dealing with, 109

Comptometer operator, job description for, 115

Computer operators, job description for, 120-121; representation of women among, 129

Computer programers, average wages for, 61, 64-65; index of segregation for, 57; occupational segregation among, 56; pay differentials for, 71; representation of women among, 128; wage differences by sex among, 72

Conant, E., 32

Cosmetrologists, female percentage of, 11

Council of Economic Advisors, 12

Data, source of, 4

153

Gross, E., 11

Hairdressers, proportion of women
among, 11
Hamilton, Mary, 46
Hammerman, H., 110
Hedge, J.N., 19
Hiring practices, 29-31; and availability of male labor, 82; of higher-
wage firms, 37; model of random
hiring, 48-52; and segregation, 75

Index, proportion-female, 87-93
Indices of segregation, 10, 12, 54-55;
actual and expected, 57; model for
computation of, 50
Industry, and proportion-female index, 95; wage and proportion-female regressions for, 88-89, 90-91,
92-93
Industry segregation, 5-6; and employer preferences, 40; example of,
8-10; and pay rates, 24; and wage
differentials, 42, 43, 44. *See also*
Segregation
Information, workers' access to, 28-29
Interfirm effect, on pay differentials,
67
Internal labor market analysis, 98-105;
application of, 100-102; policy
implications of, 104
Interoccupational segregation, 5, 42;
example of, 6-8. *See also* Segregation, occupational
Intrafirm effect, on pay differentials,
67-69
Intraoccupational segregation, 5; con-
firmation of, 73; criterion for, 48;
example of, 6-8; extent of, 52-59;
and pay differentials, 75; and wage
differentials, 42. *See also* Segregation, occupational

Job categories. *See* Occupational categories
Johnson, G.E., 31, 85

Kassalow, E.M., 93, 94

Kerr, C., 28
Keypunch operator, 115-116
Kmenta, J., 83

Labor force, women in, 18, 100. *See
also* Women; Workers
Labor markets, blue-collar, 98; discrimination in, 103; internal, 21-25;
interoccupational segregation in,
10; primary, 26; secondary, 26; sex
discrimination in, 36, 98 (*see also*
Discrimination); sex segregation in,
1 (*see also* Segregation); wage hierarchy of firms in, 95
Labor unions, and equal employment,
109-110. *See also* Unionization
Law of Large Numbers, 54
Legislation, employment, 105-108
Lester, R., 27, 29
Lewis, H., 85
Librarianship, proportion of men in,
18

Madden, J.F., 32
Managerial occupations, and differential pay rates, 25
Manicurists, proportion of women
among, 11
"Market segregation," 5
Markets, unstructured, 26. *See also*
Labor markets
Men, in higher-wage firms, 83; in integrated firms, 61, 73; in segregated
firms, 61; wage rates for, 59. *See
also* Women
Merit (ability), and employer constraints, 34; and intrafirm pay differentials, 45; and pay differentials,
23, 45; and wage differentiation,
101
Mincer, J., 46
Mobility, worker, 28-29; for women
workers, 110
Model, employee discrimination, 72;
of random hiring, 48-52
Monopolistic industries, and occupational discrimination, 41

Teachers, elementary school, changes in segregation of, 13; proportion of men among, 18

Technological change, and female employment, 24

Ticket agents, representation of women among, 17

Transcribing-machine operator, job description for, 120

Trenton, labor studies in, 29

Turnover, labor, 27; and hiring practices, 29, 34

Typists, job description for, 120; proportion of women in occupation, 8, 18

Ullman, J.C., 27

Unemployment, 110-111

Unionization, blue-collar, 93; effect on wage structure of, 102; and representation of women, 95; and wage differences, 31-32; and wage index, 87; and wage rates, 85, 95

Unions, role of, 109-110

Unit of analysis, establishment as, 2

Wachtel, H.M., 33, 36

Wage index, calculation of, 83

Wage rates, and distribution of sexes among establishments, 58-73; and employment patterns, 76-82; establishment, 82-94; and female employment, 38; and hierarchy of firms, 75; in integrated firms, 59; interfirm differences in, 60, 76; and occupational categories, 47; and ranking of firms, 37; and representation of women, 43, 84, 95; in segregated firms, 59; and sex composition of employment, 36, 102; and unionization, 93

Wage regression equation, 85

Wage structure, internal, 101; rigidity of, 35

Wages, and employer constraints, 34; and individual characteristics, 32; interfirm hierarchy of, 25-33; and internal labor market structure, 99; internal structure for, 22-23; intra-occupational sex differences in, 46; and occupational categories, 2; and proportion-female regressions, 88-89, 90, 92; in segregated vs. integrated firms, 73; white-collar vs. blue-collar, 94

Wallace, P.A., 107

Weiss, L.W., 31, 93

White-collar occupations, women in, 86

White-collar workers, pay increases for, 93

Women, absenteeism rates for, 30, 34; absorption into labor force of, 18; distribution of firms by representation of, 81; impact of level of unemployment on, 110-111; in lower-wage firms, 83; older vs. younger, 30; turnover of, 30, 34; in white-collar occupations, 86. See also Men; Proportion-female index

Workers, and pay differentials, 25-26 (see also Pay differentials); stability of, 34, 99; with unstable work patterns, 27. See also specific occupations

Working conditions, 29

About the Author

Francine D. Blau is Assistant Professor of Economics and Labor and Industrial Relations at the University of Illinois at Urbana-Champaign, where her teaching includes courses on women in the labor market. A graduate of Cornell University, she received the M.A. and Ph.D. degrees from Harvard University. Ms. Blau was a founding member of the American Economic Association Committee on the Status of Women in the Economics Profession. She was coauthor (with Adele Simons and others) of the background paper for *Exploitation from 9 to 5: Report of the Twentieth Century Fund Task Force on Women and Employment*, and has published many articles on the economic status of women.